This book is split into two sections as you will see from flipping through the pages. Part one is the story of how creativity helped save my life. Part 2 is the practical action steps you can use daily to find and nurture your own creative superhero. Just like this book, the creative process has many angles, many sides, and many surprises. My promise to you is this:

If you do the provided creativity challenge, as well the CREATE morning routine, daily for 30 days, you will transform your life in ways you could never have imagined.

My goal with this book is to share with you the tools and stories I have used to find my inner creative superhero. Creativity truly did save my life and this book is my gratitude prayer to it. My hope is that it adds value to your life and sparks a creative inferno inside you that changes the way you look at the world around you.

Edited by Keira Faer
Cover Design by Adam Wilber
Layout and Graphic Design by Branden Wolf

Adam Wilber
2017

Printed in the United States of America

This book is dedicated to the most important and beautiful things I've ever co-created: my children, Carter Blake and Alina Malia.

I wish nothing more than for you to go through life knowing your true worth. Never allow another's perception of you alter your actions or motivations. I love you both with every ounce of life I possess.

CONTENTS

CREATIVITY
The Magic Formula

"CREATIVITY IS CONTAGIOUS. PASS IT ON."

– Albert Einstein

Creativity is … an integral thread, woven tightly into the fabric of our society. The struggle is the manner in which creativity has been advertised and skewed to appear inaccessible, as though meant only for the gifted elite, or those born with a specific genetic ability. And while scientists have discovered that about two percent of the human race is born with a specified type of creativity, that in no way suggests that creativity is limited to that two percent. I don't believe so, anyway. Though it may be a bit of a mystery, creativity is absolutely everywhere, found in each and every one of us.

All we have to do is find it, harness it, and apply it to our lives. With all the technological advancements, we need creativity more than ever. The individual experience is something no technology or automation can conquer. This is because creativity is an essential, enigmatic piece that contributes to the puzzle of who we are. It's human, and random enough to exist outside of technology's advances.

The harnessing of creativity will only grow in importance as technology continues to develop and transform our society. Thus, we need to prioritize creativity so our children can access and incorporate it from the start. Just imagine how phenomenal our society would be if it was fueled by individuals who were tapped into their own creativity, openly sharing their passions with the world.

"Technology is rapidly changing the global workforce," says Elon Musk, chief executive officer and founder of Tesla, SolarCity, and SpaceX. As there will most likely be more and more job losses due to foolproof, automated machinery over the next twenty years or so, the only surefire way of securing income for yourself is to become an expert in the one thing that can't be automated: creativity.

Dallas Mavericks owner and Shark Tank judge Mark Cuban notes that "automation is going to cause unemployment, and we need to prepare for it." Musk often speaks on this point as well: he believes that computers, intelligent machines, and robots are the workforce of the future. As more of our jobs are replaced by these technologies, there will be less and less work for us to do. He foresees that humans will eventually receive sustaining payments from the government while they focus their energies on other areas, such as creative endeavors. This automation will offer us opportunities for more complex and interesting interactions with the world, and will usher in a new kind of workforce: one that is built around the individual and the creative!

By focusing on becoming a super creative person, your mind becomes your talent. All you will need to manifest success for yourself is … yourself. You can create what you desire, and I want this book to show you why and how this is all possible.

Plus, just imagine how incredible and impactful this surge of creative energy could be for our world, especially if it stemmed from epicenters across the globe! What I'm speaking of is the beginning of a global creative revolution. And I don't think it's too far out on the horizon.

I have split this book into two parts to mirror how the creative process unfolds. The creative process consists of two equally essential pieces: mental effort and physical stamina. If you're not in the right headspace, creatively speaking, then the physical will never come to fruition. And even if you are in the right headspace, but don't follow through on turning those ideas into reality, you won't have anything to show for your efforts. Just like anything else in life, the balance is key.

The first step in this process is convincing yourself that you are creative. And believe me, you are a creative individual. We each have an innate ability to transform our realities. Michael Michalko says in his incredible book, Thinkertoys, "Once you believe you are creative, you will begin to believe in the worth of your ideas, and you will have the persistence to implement them." He goes on to say, "the artist, after all, is not a special person; every person is a special kind of artist."

We all spin magic from what we see, feel, and experience in the world around us. The goal of this book is to showcase just how each and every individual is a creative. I want to lead you back to a fundamental part of who you are, using the wisdom I've found in my own journey with creativity.

After you open yourself up to the idea that you already possess limitless creativity, you need to ready your mind to exist within a playful mentality, where absolutely everything you feel, touch, or experience could turn into art. Then, once you've opened yourself to the creative and playful sides of yourself, the physical side takes hold, producing art. Beautiful, potentially life-altering art. Your art.

But art takes on so many forms. Though your creations may take shape as a poem, painting, or song, creativity is not limited to writing, fine art, and music. Creativity is more than just art… heck, art is more than just art! It can take shape as a product that

you create, patent, and sell, or it could be
a new way of thinking about communication. It
could be a fresh perspective on relationships, or merely the
new way in which you structure your day-to-day life. Creativity is
found wherever we take it; art is found wherever we make it!

This brings me back to the book layout. The white-covered side encourages your mind, whereas the black covers the actionable techniques
and steps that you can take to practice your creativity. Please delve
in and trust yourself, as well as your own creativity, as you absorb
what I have to say. My promise to you is that I have poured my
heart and soul into these pages in an effort to help its readers
find their most creative self, and in turn live their most
fulfilling and passion driven lives. Put these words to
use and I promise you will surprise yourself with
how far your own creativity will take you in
your life's journey.

FINDING CREATIVITY

*C*reativity is a conception that has eluded scientists for eons. Where does it come from? Are only some gifted with it? Do muses whisper secrets in our ears to create what has not yet been seen? I think that our minds are constantly swimming in creativity. All we need to do is embrace what we already possess, learn how to recognize it, and grab onto it!

We are meant to innovate, grow, expand, develop, and change the earth. We create instinctively. And that's what I want each of you to remember: how creativity flows in our veins and propels our lives forward in unexpected and exciting ways when we are open to it!

We don't have to fear creativity or feel that we can't possess it. There is no barrier to creative expression. As I said, creativity has been restricted to include only select forms of artistic expression developed by and from members of the ruling elite. This idea is damaging to the rest of us because it causes us to detach from a very intrinsic part of ourselves, due to the fear that our creations won't be respected or appreciated by others. Nobody wants to put their heart into something only to be told that it sucks. This was one of the biggest hurdles that I faced when trying to express my creativity. I still struggle with this. This tendency to worry about what others think has hindered me time and time again, prohibiting me from truly expressing myself.

I hear from people all around the world who tell me that they just aren't the creative type." To that, I always reply with a polite, but firm, "Bullshit!" We are all creative, all the time, and we don't even recognize it! Whenever we expand our beliefs or enrich our minds with new information, we are actively being creative. You must first convince yourself that you are creative. If you don't believe it, then it will never be your reality. By getting out of your comfort zone and not giving a shit about what others think of your work, and by being vulnerable enough to give into yourself and share your passion with the world, you can live your life in the most fulfilling way.

I've thought long and hard about when my first dance with creativity took place and I think it all stems back to the time I saw magic for the first time.

The first time I ever felt the power of magic

was when I was only six and living in Hanover, New Hampshire, with my dad and sister. I was at a friend's house, hanging out and acting a fool, like any other six-year-old, when my friend Jimmy showed me a trick: an old classic called the Silk Vanish.

First, he showed me his hands. They were empty. Then, he showcased a little, red silk scarf. He proceeded to stuff the scarf into his fist, and then he snapped his fingers. Poof! The silk vanished. I was in awe. And then he continued the trick. He snapped his fingers again, and the silk returned!

Now, I'm sure many, if not most, of you have seen this trick. I hadn't, but as intrigued as I was by it, I wasn't fooled. I knew there was a "trick" to it. I immediately called out my thoughts on the method. "That's easy. It went up your sleeve, and then you just pulled it back out of your sleeve to make it come back."

My friend Jimmy, however, was ready for my retort. He gave me a half-smile and then proceeded to roll up his sleeves very slowly and carefully. He illustrated in a no-nonsense manner that there were no devices or hidden scarves.

As I watched him do this, my mind began to race. I started to consider the idea that he might try to do the trick with his sleeves rolled up to throw me off! If he could do that... well, then, everything that my six-year-old self knew and understood about the world would be flipped-turned upside down, to say the least! I knew that there was no way he was going to make the thing vanish with his sleeves up. But I watched patiently, my doubting eyes darting over him as I waited in angst for the grand reveal.

At that point, life as I knew it was over, and now... I had found magic.

Well, of course I asked him—let's be honest, I begged him—to teach me how the trick worked. And wouldn't you know it: the little punk refused to show me the trick. I was friggin' furious! Yet, I felt more alive and full of awe than ever before. I was determined to find out how Jimmy had done it.

The next day, I approached my dad, and he happily took me to the bookstore after school to look for some books on magic. I found a book called The Klutz Book of Magic. I remember sitting there in the store, hunched up over the book, flipping furiously through it in the hopes that I would find something—anything—about a silk scarf vanishing trick. Finally, after seeming to start a small fire from the speed of my fingers as they ripped through the pages, I found the trick I was looking for at the very back of the book. My blood began to surge, and my heart started racing while I sat there, barely moving as I absorbed the secrets to the impossible. Here is where my creative spark was ignited. Here is where it all began for me. Other people may have scoffed, said "whatever," and gone on their merry way without thinking twice about the trick. But for me, this was everything. Only one day before I found myself in the bookshop, unearthing the secrets that were to become my destiny, I had been confronted with something that made me question all reason.

Since I couldn't afford the book, I read it cover to cover while my dad and sister occupied themselves. It was lucky for me that they did, because there was no way they could pull me away from that book until I was good and satisfied. On my way out of the store, I made a snap decision to "borrow" the little contraption that was necessary to make the silk vanish, as it was so neatly (and so accessibly) tucked inside the book I was reading. I knew it was wrong to do, but I couldn't help myself! My curiosity had gotten the better of me. I went home to practice the trick I had learned until I perfected it.

First, I showed my sister. BOOM! Her mind was blown, and she begged me to teach her the trick, just as I had begged Jimmy. Like him, I stood my ground and refused to tell. It was so empowering! And especially so for my six-year-old self.

After a few more practice sessions in front of the mirror, I had finally mustered up enough courage to show my dad the trick. I walked out into the living room where he was watching TV, and asked him if he would like to see some magic.

As graciously as ever, he accepted my offer, and I then proceeded to work through the motions and movements that I had just practiced, doing my absolute best not to let my excitement get the better of me. As I opened my hand to show that the silk had vanished, I could see the pride mingled with surprise, excitement, and confusion all showcase themselves on his face. I had totally fooled him! I became so excited in that moment that my hands began to shake, and I had to quickly bring the silk back before asking him if he knew how I had done it.

"It went up your sleeve," my dad pronounced in a matter-of-fact tone, echoing my own sentiments. Like father, like son. I, of course, then pulled a "Jimmy" by slowly and methodically rolling up my sleeves to show the trick again.

BOOM! I opened up my hands, and again, the scarf was gone. It was at this moment that I saw true astonishment upon my father's face—for the first time in my life.

Wow! My dad is baffled, I thought, as I stood frozen in awe. This was the best moment of my life. I felt so full, and experienced such a surge of wisdom, power, and desire to harness untapped secrets. The feeling was electrifying. All of a sudden, I found myself obsessed with magic, and began spending all of my time thinking and learning about it.

Over the course of the next twenty-some years, I continued to practice, perform, learn, and create magic. And I have no intention of stopping anytime soon.

That moment in my childhood set me on the course for the rest of my life. I didn't know it all then, and I couldn't expect myself to have understood, but this was my passion. Sometimes we just live our lives with passion without ever labeling or recognizing what it is.

And that is something I want you to consider and remember. What is it that drives you forward? It could be anything at all. As you consider what this could be, go back and try to recall what electrified your curiosity—what sparked an interest inside of you. Do you remember the last time you felt full of wonder? Can you envision yourself in a situation where all you want to do is learn and absorb everything about it?

Seeing a successful magic trick performed in front of your eyes almost forces you to slow down and pay attention to what you might be missing. Just as Ferris said on his infamous day off, "Life moves pretty fast. If you don't stop to look around once in a while, you could miss it." Well, magic moves fast, too. If you don't give the trick your full attention, it'll get you, and you'll miss it.

This same thing goes for all creative endeavors. When we find our interests ignited, we focus our attention, and dig in to the wonder of what we don't yet comprehend. It is when we dig our feet into life like this that we're really living. Our creativity allows us to live in the moment shamelessly, consumed by our own concocted version of reality.

THE SPARK

Creativity is not talent. Talent is an innate ability, but creativity is a mere manner of operating. Unlike talent, which is particular to each individual, creativity is in us all. We simply have to get ourselves into the right frame of mind for the creativity to flow naturally. Creativity is completely unrelated to abilities or intelligence. Creativity is emotional, aware, and receptive. Creativity is alive, as though it has a voice of its own!

Creativity is a state of play, and is only possible when the mind is open to it. The dictionary defines play as: "engage in activity for the enjoyment and recreation rather than a serious or practical purpose". This is not to say that to get your mind into a creative state you must only do so for recreation and without purpose but rather that you must be able to put your mind into a space it can play like a child with any, and all the ideas it dreams up. Don't let being an adult block you from your ideas and the journey they will lead you on. While in your creative mode you can't worry about what others think of your creative process or it's end outcome, you must be OK to just play.

We must relinquish our stronghold on the realities of our lives to allow the playful state to come through. You see, "stress and creation do not sustain one another." John Cleese, one of my sources of inspiration when it comes to creativity, shared this idea during one of his speeches as a means of encouragement to others in letting their creativity flow.

The spark of inspiration comes most often when we are in this state of play. This is exactly why so many artists consider themselves "dreamers." They spend most of their lives in this constant state of play, where they remain somewhat separated from reality. However, constant playtime can be quite detrimental when one has to face the realities of everyday life. So, I am most certainly not saying that you should hop in your car, throw your responsibilities out the window, and drive forward without direction. Rather, to reach this playful mindset, find a method or ritual that allows you to transition from this play-state to a more responsible state of focused attention easily. The balance between the two is key.

In releasing our fears and anxieties, we become our true selves. When we allow vital life energy to flow through us, and we refrain from getting in its way, there can be no tension, and thus, nothing blocking us from our potential. When we allow life to happen to us, and we can meet it with joy, grace, happiness, gratefulness, and most importantly, creativity, we no longer find ourselves blocked by the fears and anxieties that inhibit positive momentum. We find a more natural flow that applies to every aspect of our lives!

We need to be open when pondering our possibilities; but we are only efficient when we commit to the choices we make. This is where many who call themselves creatives make a wrong turn. They continue with openness and self-doubt for much too long, far past the time when they should've stopped the criticism to make way for the confidence.

Not that I'm one to talk. I let far too much time pass me by before I fully embraced my own creativity. I lived the life of a drifter until I was about thirty. I was spending my time smoking herb, partying, and not really sinking my teeth into anything in the world around me. Though I was always creating magic tricks and routines to show my friends, I never really considered myself creative. I didn't even think of myself as intelligent. I didn't feel that I had much purpose at all, outside getting by in the day to day. I was not fulfilled, and deep down, I was feeling that tug for something more. I'm sure I'd been feeling that tug for years in some way or another, but now it was speaking up, and at a volume I could hear.

Then, a short time after I turned thirty, I felt the spark: the spark of inspiration and inner confidence. It surged through me, but in a subtle way, as though a soft voice was urging me forward.

Some soul searching led me to ask myself the more difficult questions, like what I wanted to do, what my primary motivations were, and where my passion was. I also asked myself what I would choose to do every day, if money were no issue. After each and every one of these questions, that little voice whispered "magic." Though I had always known it, the fact I wanted to create and share magic. I could say it proudly now. I wanted to make magic. Maybe I didn't consider myself a creative. Maybe I doubted whether I would be successful. But it didn't matter—once I felt that spark, I knew I had to do something about it.

So, I decided to follow the instinct, and the subtle surge of creative energy. I decided to send a trick submission to the world's largest magic magazine, aptly called Magic Magazine.

Magic magazine dedicates a section of its publication to readers' tricks and ideas. I had created a trick many years earlier, but I thought, what the hell…It can't hurt to send it, and it'd be pretty cool if they accepted it. So off it went. I didn't even think about it twice. I just wrote it up, sent it in, said "screw it," and forgot about it.

After not hearing from them for a while, I assumed that it wasn't creative enough. I was moving on with my life when they finally did contact me. After about two months, they called to tell me how much they loved my trick, and that they wanted to publish it in their magazine. I was pumped! I still didn't quite feel like I was a creative, but it felt damn good to see my trick in print. The magazine had given me some feedback in the process, as well. They told me how original my approach was to the classic trick I patterned mine after called Bill Transpo. The trick I submitted was called Cash Card. It goes like this: show the audience a playing card to prove it was real, and immediately turn it into a dollar bill. Now, this wasn't a crazy idea , and it really was only a modified version of a very classic trick. But my improvements allowed the magician to show the bill on both the front and back side, something you couldn't do with the original method.

I thought, Original? Me? My idea? Alright, alright. This was something I needed to follow. I finally felt like I had direction. I had finally found something that worked, and I was being noticed. The magazine trick success, along with my soul searching and the inner confidence I was gaining somewhat, gave me the push and the focus I needed to allow creativity to start to really flow. It offered me the opportunity to start taking myself seriously as a creator and magician.

So often, we only find the push we need once we get noticed. As unfortunate as it is, feedback does help us focus. Kiki Smith, a world-renowned artist, said, "Just do your work. And if the world needs your work, it will come and get you. And if it doesn't, do your work anyway." The great thing is, once you do open yourself up, whether because of external positive feedback or not, you-all of a sudden-have something to push against! The creativity continues to fuel and feed you, so long as you commit to it with an open mind.

So, the world was finally starting to want my work, and I was awakening to it. After my trick was published in Magic Magazine that first month, people began to notice me, and contact me to lecture and perform, which really pushed me forward creatively.

Then, very slowly, I started hearing from people who had read the trick and loved it. The more and more I spoke with these people, the more I was hearing how creative the trick was, until someone actually asked me about my creative process. Now, something about that question really intrigued me. It was such an amazing feeling to have someone not only appreciate my work, but wanting to know how I worked. It was as though I was hit with lighting, and then, when I got up afterwards, I suddenly had some creative

power! Well, I wanted nothing more than to nurture that creativity as best I could and become a creative powerhouse. I started writing down every magic trick I could think of. I started building a morning routine that focused on making creativity the focus of my mind and actions.

My point is this: it wasn't until I was thirty years old that I finally realized I was creative., and all it took was sending a simple trick to a magazine. The spark of that first (albeit minor) success inspired me to sell my creations to Ellusionist, the world's largest online magic store. A short while later, I was hired by that same company and quickly rose to become the general manager while inventing some of the all-time best selling magic tricks. Plus, all the while, I got to do what I love, which is make magic! And what got me there? My creativity. And what exactly helped me find my creativity? My purpose? My success? Ritual. My morning ritual helped me open up to all of these possibilities and more. My morning ritual helped me to see what was possible for me, and what steps I could take to get to where I wanted.

For so long, I had no idea what my calling was. Though in the secret pocket of my heart, and in the war-torn pages of my mind, I viewed magic with a sense of reverence and love, I had absolutely no idea how to manifest a life for myself where I got to make magic and make a living from it. I had no clue as to how to actualize my secret dreams and desires.

Once It came down to it, all I needed to do was become comfortable with failure and continuously create, no matter what. After the success of my first trick in Magic Magazine, I began posting more of my tricks on Ellusionist's Facebook page and even submitted one to a contest they were running. I was so sure that I would win the contest, as I felt that my trick was not only badass but original, and a real fooler. However, when I didn't even make the top three, I was confused, frustrated, angry, and full of doubt. Immediately, I started to lose faith in my creativity. Due to external opinions, my confidence faltered. My audience facilitates my success, after all! If they don't love it, then am I really just an arrogant, overly confident fraud?

So much self-doubt circulated through my mind regarding my magic. I was grasping at straws to find my center again and really encouraged myself through my rituals. I threw my efforts into engaging on Ellusionist's Facebook page and their active members forum and drawing as much attention to my name as I could. After a month, I got a call from someone who worked at Ellusionist. They asked me if I would be willing to release my trick for sale on their website—the trick I thought was a dud because it didn't win! What they told me was that my trick was really too good for them to place in the contest, so they hoped I might like to sell it for a profit instead.

Boom! Just like that, I was back. I just knew that trick was good. I was really just starting to trust my instincts when that perceived failure threw me off and rattled my cages. And then, to discover that there was actually no failure at all! Well, I used that momentum to surge forward again. But this time, I progressed without the self-doubt that had been taking up space in my mind. I learned my lesson. Trust your instincts, and don't allow failure to rip you to shreds. Keep your momentum!

I kept working on tricks to build a name for myself with Ellusionist. After a time, I started to consider how amazing it'd be to actually make a living from my passion. But, this idea was insane to me, so I put all expectation aside. At the time, I was working some odd jobs that really didn't fulfill me to support my creative inclinations. All the while, tons of people were messaging me through

Ellusionist's Facebook page, and I was really gaining quite a following. The company began to take notice of the traction I was making and offered me a full-time position, without my own inquiry!

I hope to use my story of finding my purpose through creativity to inspire you to do the same! I hope you can believe in yourself and release all the doubts, fears, and anxieties that keep you exiled from your true self. I hope you can learn how to incorporate creativity into each and every aspect of your life, as I have. Without the original spark, and then birth of my creative awareness, I never would have been able to find myself now, where I am, living my dreams by creating magic and supporting an entire, beautiful family from the profits.

THE CREATIVE RITUAL

*R*itual is everything! Throughout history, records show of tribes engaging in ritual. Ritual bonds us together and makes magic from our combined energy. When we use ritual or routine as a practice to open our minds to our innate creativity, we are more likely to access what is already flowing through us on a regular basis. When we prepare our minds, we are able to facilitate the flow of creative energy.

In order to get yourself into a more open mindset that is ready for play, you need time and space. You need time away from your normal life and space from your daily demands. It's best if you can create an oasis for yourself, where you can safely escape your realities and allow the mind to open. One way of doing this is to set a timer, so that you can allow the current of creativity, and continue it unimpeded by any thoughts of time or duties. For, you see, time and space don't always function the same way when we are in the mode of creative expression.

I suggest that you set aside anywhere from forty-five to ninety minutes for creative play every day. Anything less, and you may not see results; any more, and you may burn out. Sometimes, you may experience a burst of creativity that lasts for hours or days on end. When you find yourself in this flow, you can and certainly should ride the wave of creative energy.

Just as our conscious dream state allows for ideas to incubate, dreaming can nurture our creative expressions and ideas. Imaginative time can function somewhat like dreaming, as it allows for a lack of structure to encourage fresh ideas to rise to the surface. This is why the routines work. They do not merely isolate a moment of time for you to be creative. No, they expand your horizons, then bleed over into other areas of your life, inspiring creative solutions and turning problems into opportunities.

Our neurons fire like mad when we're in this play state (or when we're dreaming), and especially so when we are without the hindrances of our day-to-day troubles, responsibilities and to-do lists. When the ritual's only purpose is to allow for creativity, the creative muscles are stretched and eventually strength-ened. With this isolation of creativity comes more confidence and commitment to our own creative expressions, and as we continue to practice our creativity, it only grows stronger!

When we know we can do something, the task becomes a helluva lot easier to tackle. Confidence helps here. And when we commit to the task, we commit to finding the answer. Just like a rabbit, we burrow until the best solution is found. Creativity is only benefitted by commitment. When we refuse to settle for the first solution we find, we refuse to let our creativity go to waste. We honor our creativity by tolerating the slight discomforts that bring us to our ultimate results.

And what's more, when we can do this all with humor in our hearts! Humor readily brings us into the open mindset by helping to free us from sadness, as well as the pull of our selfish ego. True humor is the ultimate genius in creativity, and especially so when coupled with awareness. Yes, yes, yes—comedy is central to creative problem-solving. When we take things with a jolly attitude, we allow for the energy to continue to flow, rather than block it off with sadness or fear.

You may ask yourself, If humor is so important to creativity, then why are so many creative artists known to be depressed? Well, humor is not the answer to creativity, but rather a tool that allows you to access creativity. It's not the only tool, either. Humor is merely one of the most direct ways of accessing creativity because of how it allows connections to be made. When you approach things with humor, you take the weight and worry out of the idea, problem, or creation, and allow for more, fun, unique, and creative solutions.

Now, I'm going to introduce you to my morning routine. I think of it as a skeleton, which each individual can customize their personal rituals. My routine is comprised of six different steps. I could tackle them all in an hour, or even just five minutes. You dig in deeper the more time you spend with them. But still, committing to doing the same routine each day for even just five minutes could change your life.

The evidence that those individuals who stick to a morning routine tend to be much more creative and successful overall is beyond overwhelming, and what I am presenting, isn't really all that new! I have merely streamlined a process that opens the mind to creativity and worked out all the bugs that stand in the way.

These steps definitely do not need to be performed in the order I've suggested! A slight variation may benefit your own practice, as it does mine. If you do change the order, I do recommend, you avoid eating until the very end. Your mind is so much more open before you eat. Also, I do recommend you start off with a large glass of water and one tablespoon of apple cider vinegar, to hydrate and help clear out any residual negativity.

So, here is the ritual:

1. CLEAR YOUR HEAD
2. READ
3. EXERCISE
4. ASHTANGA
5. TESTIMONIALS
6. EAT

CLEAR YOUR HEAD

*T*he first thing I do when I wake up is my morning meditation. I'm sure I don't have to tell you the benefits of meditation. But, if you are not familiar with the outrageous amount of positive benefits that are directly linked to a daily practice of meditation, spend the next fifteen minutes on Google, and I assure you that you'll quickly understand why I make this the first part of every day. I spend anywhere from three to twenty-five minutes meditating, with a focus on creativity. I do this with the use of a guided meditation audio track, which is included with this book! You can access it at: www.adamwilber.com/create.

Any sort of meditation will work. What's important is the mindfulness and focus that come from the daily practice. I know that meditation can be a scary and frustrating beast to those who have never tried, or who have tried with little success. That is why I've added a simple beginner's guide to meditation that can be downloaded for free as well.

These guided meditations will kick start your journey into the wonderful world of mindfulness with a focus on finding your inner creativity in a busy and hectic world.

READ

I am dyslexic (I know, I know … woe is me), but I didn't know anything about it until I was twenty-seven years old. All through school, I just thought I couldn't read well. So, I became the funny guy and made excuses when I was called on in class to read aloud. I could read, but only very slowly, and I felt like a fool doing so in front of other people. I now believe that this forced me to be creative and to find a creative way to solve my problems, only I never saw it that way.

As reading is so difficult for me, I am a huge audiobook junkie. I listen to anywhere from ten to twenty books a month, and many of them I will listen to multiple times in a row. I do believe that hearing a book and reading it are not the same. I have found that sometimes you need to listen to a book multiple times to absorb the same amount of information you would have if you had actually read it.

That being said, a lot of the books out there are shit, and audiobooks seem to be a good way to sift through the crap and focus in on the gold you come across. Reading is so important for so many reasons. But since you're reading this, you most likely already feel this way!

In my routine, I always try to read or listen to something that will inspire a childlike mindset for the day, something that will either inspire or educate me about new ideas that I can use in my creative life. I then store these ideas in the back of my mind for when they decide to show up, riding towards me upon the back of inspiration. Yes, that's right. I have a giant library of ideas stored away, but as my mind is always so open and receptive, these ideas are always accessible! If an idea hits me that particularly inspires me, I will grab my iPhone and write it in my notes app. I then revisit these notes every week to see what floats to the surface. I don't say this to sound boisterous but rather to let you know, If I can keep my head filled with an army of ideas to use when creatively

necessary then by all means, so can you!

It's said that you are the average of the five people you spend the most time with. Well, as I grew up living in the backwoods of New England, I had no idea where to look for these five people. I wanted to find these people badly so that I could be inspired and motivated by them. One day, I read in a book that all you really needed to do was surround yourself with the ideas and stories of those five people to receive the exact same benefits. I say: go find out who your top five people are! Are they professionals in your field or friends? Authors, creatives, inventors … whatever and whomever they are, go find them and seek out their wisdom

They may have some sort of literature supporting their endeavors. If they are just a friend, record some creative conversations or conduct an interview with them. What would be great is if you could find and listen to the audiobooks of the people you ultimately want to surround yourself with! You don't have to be friends with or even be in the same room with these people to surround yourself with their thoughts and ideas. This small piece of advice has been worth its weight in gold for me, both in my life and career, and I hope it can be the same for you in yours.

EXERCISE

*T*he third thing I delve into is exercise. Once again, no secret here! Those who exercise every day live better lives. It's that simple. I do twenty minutes of cardio, and then fifteen minutes of body weight exercises, all the while listening to my audiobooks. I get two things done at the same time, and the combination of the two helps me focus. Perhaps the activity keeps my mind from wandering so much, thus allowing me to concentrate on the book and its ideas. With the Audible app I use to listen to audiobooks, you can quickly make notes when something sparks your interest. So, you can come back to it after your workout if you want to dive deeper or jot down your personal notes on the topic.

If you conduct a strenuous workout, lift heavy weights, or take a yoga class, then you will of course have to separate the two experiences. However, the combination really does help me to not only focus, but also make the most of my time! And our time is our most valuable commodity!

ASHTANGA

*A*shtanga is my chosen form of yoga. When it comes to yoga, there are more bencfits than I could ever list, so I won't even begin to try. The key benefit for our purposes is the grounding and centering you experience when you commit to the form. I generally spend fifteen or twenty minutes of my day on yoga, though I generally want to stay much longer. Some days, I will forego exercise and, instead, spend forty-five minutes to an hour practicing yoga. If you're unfamiliar with yoga, you can try some stretching that really gets you grounded. Start on the ground and think about your bones sinking into the earth as you raise your spirit towards the sky. Focus on your breath here, allowing you to become more grounded with each inhalation, and your spirit to rise higher with every exhalation. I know, it may seem counterintuitive, but dichotomies work, and they really help us to stretch not only our mindset, but our creativity! You can download a free seven-day yoga practice from my website that I had developed specifically to boost your inner creativity. It's a beginner/intermediate plan that will get you feeling the benefits of a daily yoga practice.

TESTIMONIALS

Testimonials serve as my way of focusing on gratitude. I write three testimonials each day. These can be for a friend of mine, my children, a great meal I had … anything that I choose to be grateful for that day. I put my thoughts down on paper, writing almost as though I were trying to write the best damn Yelp review of all time.

When we focus on gratitude each morning, it really benefits our emotional, physical, and spiritual well-being. Scientists have studied the astounding effects of gratitude on the human nature. Gratitude improves not only our moods, energy levels, and sleep, but also boosts our immune systems, and helps to keep our stress at a minimum!

For a while, I used to say prayers of gratitude to myself, but I found I would rush through them, and I wouldn't really allow for the gratitude to fulfill me at all. That whole method became a bit stale for me, so I decided to write them as testimonials. And boy, has it ever been life-changing! Something in the process helps me to specify exactly what it is that I'm grateful for, which then grants me this eye-opening sense of clarity. Honestly, it's magical! I so love the depth of experience when I express myself in this way, and I am quite proud of the methodological discovery, as well! Though the difference between silent prayers and written testimonials may seem subtle, it has been an absolute game changer for my life.

I have also, on occasion, written these testimonials to share with others. Though it's such a simple way of showing the people in your life how important they are to you, there really is something special about showing another person the importance of the role that they play in your life. I don't recommend writing these testimonials with the intention of handing them out, but when the mood strikes you, why not make someone's day by letting them know how much of a kick-ass human being they really are!

EAT

Since the morning routine is done … eat! You have just spent the first part of your day nurturing your body and mind, and now you can eat something healthy that replenishes you, getting you ready to kill it during your day.

I have included a simple, seven-day meal plan that focuses on power foods to fuel your body and mind. I can't stress the importance of eating the right foods enough. It's been said a million times before-and for good reason-that you are what you eat. The nice thing about starting each day with a healthy morning routine is that by the time breakfast rolls around, you will want to fill your mind and body with proper nourishment to keep the flow of positive juju rushing through your veins.

I swear by the CREATE Morning Routine. Though it can and should be adjusted to suit your needs, you should do your best to weave it into your everyday routine. The key is to stick with it. Don't make excuses, and do it before you can talk yourself out of it. Isn't that the running runner's joke, anyway? They commit themselves to going on a run so early in the morning that they can't talk themselves out of it? Well, anyways, now it's up to you to implement this routine into your daily life, and start fueling your creativity! You have all the tools you need, now it's up to you to find the motivation to put them into practice.

Now that I've shown and explained my morning ritual, and touted its success, I want to share a personal story of falling away from the routine, and then, ultimately, finding my way back. For the last few months, I have been developing a new product that pushes past the confines of the magic world. I had hoped to create an object that would connect me to a broader audience outside the realm of magic, as much as I do love spending a majority of my time within that world.

The idea was the Fiddlestick. As I first began to craft this new idea, I was hit with a stroke of negativity. I fell out of my morning routine and was struggling to find my creativity. But you know what? That's alright. For some reason, I must have needed to allow for the tide to pass. And sometimes, we need to lose track of who we are in order to find ourselves again. Plus, when we do drift away from what we've known for a little while, it often allows for us to find a new perspective, or gain some fresh wisdom about our life choices.

So, anyways, I was really stuck in this negative slump for a while, and wasn't really producing anything too creative. I had stopped practicing what I so love to preach, and was stuck in a more close-minded state. After a while, I managed to burrow my way back out of the negative slump, but only after I had begun to implement my morning routine once again.

Slowly, I noticed the humor and the joy, and the play begin to seep back into my life, as my perspective broadened before my eyes. Instead of seeing problems and feeling bound, I began to see the play of endless possibilities, and I allowed myself to open to the world. I was in the play state, actively writing down all the ideas that flowed through my mind. Then late one night, I was awoken by this one, very strong idea. I bolted out of bed, grabbed the pen and paper I keep by my nightstand, and scribbled my thoughts down. I mean, at that hour, who even knows if I should legally be allowed to operate a pen? But, there I was.

The thing is, dreaming and daydreaming connect us more to what hovers just below the surface of our conscious self. This connection, then, tends to fire up the neurons that allow us access to subtler solutions to our problems. So much of our creativity arises when we are in a sleepy or dreamy state, as we are so much more naturally in the open-minded, playful state. You see, openness allows for opportunity. This is why I practice the advice of Jerry Seinfeld, who says he keeps a notepad by his bed at all times. I have come up with some of my best ideas in the middle of the night.

After I awoke the next morning to find my idea scribbled haphazardly, I quickly got to work. Absolutely everyone has had a multi-million-dollar idea, if not several. Writing down our ideas aligns us with our creative play state. I cannot stress enough how essential it is to write down your creative ideas. Wait, just one more time: Write Down Your Ideas. If you write down your thoughts, you recognize the ideas as worthy of remembering. This is an important first step. Just as in meditation, you want to recognize your thoughts and then release them, rather than carry them with you. Any time that you think you've got a creative idea, jot it down someplace. Perhaps, keep a recorder on you, and speak your ideas into your device. Just about every smartphone on the planet has multiple ways to jot ideas down and keep record of them easily. Practice this technique with the thoughts that flow through your head. Perhaps, make a weekly appointment with yourself to go through all the creative thoughts you've jotted down. Then, when one strikes your fancy further, you know that it's the one you're meant to explore!

Jotting down your ideas is key. In simply jotting down your ideas without analysis, you allow for your creativity to speak to you freely! And all you really need is one idea. Everything falls into place in surprising ways, once you do find yourself with a good one!

Every failure I've encountered on my creative

journey has brought me one step closer towards success! Whether a 3D print went awry, or an idea had already taken, the perceived setback only stood to reduce the options in front of me, thus streamlining my pathway towards eventual success. So even when it's a "failure," just choose to see it as a step closer toward success. Don't get bogged down, and have faith. Creativity takes faith. In trusting in the process of creativity, I know and accept each failure that comes my way as a means of showing me something that I previously overlooked.

Shit happens. Sometimes we falter. Sometimes we fall out of the routine. In my experience, when I did falter, and then went back to my routine, voilà! There was my invention! There was my creativity again. The ritual brought it back, and in the form of the Fiddlestick! I cannot speak highly enough of rituals. Whether you adapt my routine or develop your own, try it out!

WHAT WORKED FOR ME

*D*elving a bit deeper into a few of the more successful products I've created, I notice just how individual the creative process can be. The process I went through to accomplish each varies quite a lot. Though the processes I went through were so different from one another, each trick was considered a success. The only commonality here, again, is this: the routine! I know—need I repeat myself? I only do to really drive this point home: turning a focused morning routine into a daily habit will have a positive impact on your life more than any other single action you can do. (Check out the 30-day challenge to get you started at www.adamwilber.com/create)

Creativity plays just as much a role in creation as we do. Our conscious selves are accompanied by another voice: that of creativity. We are privy to the currents of creativity that run through us like bullet trains. What we capture and communicate to the rest of the world is what defines us.

Sometimes these strong currents of creativity that captivate us also take us off course. This is by far the most frustrating piece of the puzzle—a puzzle that has overcome many creatives of the past. We must bring patience to the table whenever we deal with creativity. We must trust the creative current, trust most importantly—in ourselves, and allow our perceptions of "getting off course" to fade away. We need not compare our creative currents to the rest of the world. That is the beauty of creativity: its originality.

Even when you find out, amidst your research and development, that someone else has already made what you were hoping to craft yourself, you can take comfort in knowing that their product is not your idea. Ideas are just ideas. Products are completely different. In creativity, you probably never end up where you started. More than likely, creativity twisted and torqued you in trying ways, asking from you what you could never have anticipated.

But this is exactly why so many choose the path most traveled. The fear of the unknown can be a lot to absorb on the regular, especially if the realities of your livelihood are underdeveloped. We always think that once we have all our basic necessities covered, then we will have the time for creativity. But that's the thing: even once you have all your needs covered and money in the bank, you won't know

creativity. This is purely because creativity is not something we put on the shelf, or hold off on. Creativity is not something we save away for a rainy day (or for when we make our millions). These are illusions. Creativity is now. Creativity is you, here, in this moment. What will you make of it? Who am I to know? That's entirely for you to decide.

My point is, don't wait to ignite your creative fire. I promise you that with just a little bit of faith and patience, you will see how applicable creativity is to our everyday! The Japanese have this concept of habit-forming, known in their culture as kaizen. The belief is that you practice a new habit, skill, or the like for only one minute every day. Without focusing on the future, you complete the task for one whole minute. One teensy, weensy minute. If you cannot perform an action for a whole minute with focused attention, then you will likely never acquire that skill. After all, we all know how daunting a "thirty-minute workout" is after we've been neglecting our bodies for a little while. Working up to those goals is really the only way we grow; and the only way we can naturally form new habits, mindsets, or constructs of consciousness.

Now, some of the magic that I have creatcd has come to me in a "eureka!" sort of way. You know, where absolutely everything fits, it looks perfect after just a little bit of critical development, and you're good to go. In those moments, I feel as though I am merely the conduit of the creation as though the current flows through me, and I merely facilitate an open space for it to work its magic. I love those moments, when it feels like I'm surfing a wave of creativity, as though I caught it perfectly, and now I just maintain stability and follow the flow to completion.

There is a lot of talk going around nowadays about being in the "flow state" and how we can train our minds to find this state more readily. I find the actions that lead to this flow state come while I'm at my highest level of childlike play, with very little stress or anxiety surrounding me. This is not to say that every time I goof around I'm hit with some sort of creative epiphany, but rather that the more ways I find to play and enjoy life, without life's bullshit weighing me down, the more likely I am to hit a state of flow and ride it into something truly unique and personal.

Other times, it's as though I've missed the wave, or just didn't quite capture the current

In these moments, there's usually a lot of to and fro, a great deal of "lost time", and oh so much tinkering! So many moments of trial and error. I don't let these projects get me down; I don't cower under their stubborn, struggling gaze. I fight. These are the moments I'm called to action, to either fight or surrender. When I surrender, I lose nothing, but I also gain nothing. When I continue to fight, and come back, over and over again, to face the same battle, and I win... Oh boy, do I win! These are the moments worth surviving for. These are the moments that allow us to truly thrive! When we refuse to surrender, and carry onward with a stalwart heart and with trust as our shield, we win so much more than we ever could have, had the victory been handed to us. We receive so much more—gratitude, pride, growth, allowance, understanding, and preparation. Just as in life's emotional struggles, we benefit by bringing ourselves to the battle so much more than when we try to avoid it.

25

PYRO

*T*his invention began as an endeavor toward a perceived necessity. When I had first started working for Ellusionist, I tried to consider what I could make that would solidify my position, sell well, and bring attention to my name within the company. I also wanted to gain recognition in the magic world as an inventor.

I took some time to sit down and "think tank," considering what could be universally appealing to professional magicians, hobbyists, amateurs, beginners, and those who love mysterious gadgets and toys. I wrote out a mind map, recording absolutely every idea that came to mind, and then taped it on the wall. The final outcome was this: the feeling of being a superhero—or desiring to be one—is universal. Creating such a broadly appealing product would have to be a success, if executed properly.

So once I began thinking about superheroes, I asked myself what I could give people that would give them the feeling or at least the illusion of being a superhero with real powers. Fire was, over and above, the most prevalent thought in my mind. Fire is of universal appeal, with a mesmerizing magic all on its own. If I could just figure out a way to manifest the illusion of harnessing the power of fire, I figured I would have a grand slam.

From there on out, I knew my goal: I wanted to make a product that would give people the superhuman power of fire. I was man discovering fire, all over again. I was researching (the next stage in my creative process) what was out there, who had attempted to tackle the problem before, what was out there for me to learn from and improve upon, as well as what ideas I could piggyback off to help me hasten toward my destination. But I also wanted to be very clear about what the end goal would be. I had to stay clear on the vision once I had it.

In my research, I found the things that already existed in the magic community, such as handheld devices that shoot fireballs and flash paper cannons. I realized then how broad my idea was. I needed to narrow it. I decided that what I specifically wanted was for people to be able to safely shoot fireballs, while showing their hands were completely empty. That was my target. That target came through my research of seeing what was already out there, and what was not. And now that I had my target, as well as my research, I combined the two in another mind map session.

I asked myself pointed questions, such as: what pieces of the already existing handheld devices could I use, and how could I edit them to achieve my desired result. I wrote down my thoughts rapidly in response. Then I began to tinker with the actual object. The open, playful mode of creation swept through me like a warm breeze. The nice thing about this open state of mind is that there really can be parameters, like a game where you make up all the rules, or perhaps you nix the rules completely!

Anyways, I had purchased a few hundred dollars' worth of fire-shooting toys, as well as some other props that I thought could be of use. Then, I started playing with different pieces combined together to see what worked well and what didn't. After I finally got to the point of having a very rough prototype to work with, I sought out other experts for collaboration.

By taking all the toys I purchased and combining the different elements together, I even surprised myself in what arose. By loosening up my presumptions of what could be and allowing for trial and error, I was open enough to eventually find the right solution. And it was my creative intuition that slid into place, once the right combination came about. I saw new ideas form like magic before my eyes from what already existed. These surprising juxtapositions generated new ideas, and ultimately, a new creation. Solving cognitive dissonance is creativity. And this, my friends, is what magic is all about!

Once I was ready, I took my prototype to those whom I thought possessed the expertise needed to develop my idea. There was a first collaborator who fell a little short, but I didn't lose hope. I found a second who was able to deliver the product just as I had hoped: hands-free, thin, and weightless with a sturdy safety button. I had my working prototype!

By then, it had taken me about a year and a half to move from the ideation phase to a final, working product. Mind you, I was only working on the design part-time, as I had held my position at Ellusionist since before the idea sparked. Over this year and a half, I moved from ideation, to research and development, then to prototyping, and finally to the collaboration that produced my desired result. The collaboration took around six months of a steady back-and-forth, trial-and-error process between myself and the others.

I consider this process of creation to be somewhat universal. Whether you're writing something, sculpting, drawing ... whatever it is, the process applies. Feedback, then reworking, prototyping, trial and error, and then the final product. And don't get me wrong, throughout the process there were many hurdles and obstacles. So many people told me that they thought I was crazy, and that what I was trying to do was stupid. They said it wouldn't work, it was too crazy, too expensive, too dangerous ... blah, blah, blah. Mental chatter like this only stands to get in your way.

The challenge here is just getting out of your own head and pushing through. And that could very well mean taking a break from the project for a month or so, thus giving enough space to come back with fresh eyes. A fresh mind helps you to see the project from other perspectives. However, throughout that break, I still focused on the idea, mulling over it as I practiced my morning meditations, visualizations, and things of that nature.

I was always focused on finding a solution. Every day, I would say to myself, Today, I'm going to focus my energy on being receptive to the solutions that may put themselves in front of me to solve this problem with Pyro. I would just keep it at the forefront of my mind as I moved through the world. And that's what you can do as well. Say to yourself, I'm going to find the solution to this. Perhaps

take thirty minutes or so to actively think of solutions, and record them in a mind map. Then, return to the idea when you are ready, and apply your freshly gained wisdoms.

I'm happy to say that Pyro went on to be one of the best-selling magic tricks of all time, grossing millions of dollars in sales, and introducing tens of thousands of new customers to Ellusionist and to the art of magic as a whole. If you'd like to see Pyro in more detail you will find specs & videos about it on the webpage linked earlier in this book.

DECIBEL

*D*ecibel was a completely different approach. Right away, I knew exactly what I wanted to have happen. Only, I had no research or reference point, as nothing like it had ever been made. This was tough, but it was also exciting.

I wanted to be able to play any song through a borrowed set of headphones by doing nothing more than touching the tip of the cord with my thumb and index finger. I wanted to find a way (in the spectator's mind, at least) to take the energy of their thought of a song and run it like an electrical current through my body, out my fingers, and into their own headphones. Lofty goal for sure, but it would be so badass to pull it off!

I went through many, many different versions before landing on what eventually worked. But as this creative process unfolded, I was able to skip the ideation and research phases, for the most part.

I spent about a year developing different ideas—all in vain—as I tried to find a solution. And to get those ideas, I would mind map! There are countless places to find good mind mapping tips and tricks but for me I try to keep it as simple as possible by just writing down any ideas that came to mind on index cards. Then I stick the cards to the wall in my office and pin yarn to the ones I feel pair well together. I like the feel of my wall looking like an FBI agents office who's just about to crack the biggest case of their career. Then I would try out some new ideas, experience more failure, and start the mind mapping once more.

With an idea this impossible, I figure my diligence in this process was the only thing that kept it within the realm of possibility! Each time I went back to the drawing board, I took what I learned from my failures and incorporated them into my new mind map. And sometimes the failures were only half failures, where I could use the successes, even when they were minor, to help me along my way.

I generally find that a narrower focus helps while you are actually implementing your ideas, but that the more broad-range view is even more helpful when you find yourself faced with a difficult idea. Attack your ideas, not with tunnel vision, but rather with that oh-so- wide-open mind!

One day, shortly after I hit the one-year anniversary of my idea, I got lucky. Or perhaps, I just attracted the answer to myself with all my determination! I never let the idea stray too far from the forefront of my mind, in any case. I was chatting with a musician when I brought up my trick idea. I began to explain it to him, when he said, "Oh, cool … yeah, all you should have to do is cut a headphone jack in half, and just make sure that it's small enough."

Aha! And there it was. My eureka moment; my solution. This conversation brought Decibel to where it is today. Before speaking to my friend I had never considered that I could cut a headphone jack in half and still have it play the music. Having the full rounded female piece of a headphone jack was just too big and bulky and in turn became the major design problem I had been facing. Once that initial solution of cutting the headphone jack in half was there, everything else just fell into place. I attached a Bluetooth receiver to the headphone jack, Then added a small rechargeable battery and we were off to the races.

So now I was left with a small device that would allow me to play songs through a headphone by just touching the cord to it. The next challenge was how to hide this little device in plain sight. I brainstormed on it, writing down my thoughts as they flowed through me. Eventually I came to my final solution: I would put a small piece of fake skin over the top of the headphone jack and camouflage the entire unit to look like my thumb, an old trick magicians have been using for over 60 years. The cool thing was this prop had normally been used to hide silks, and dollar bills but I decided to use it to hide the electronic device that allowed Decibel to become a reality. I took something as old as the hills and modernized it to suit my needs.

After this, I tinkered around with some Motorola head units, cutting the speaker part in half. I was playing, acting like a kid, and totally okay with failing. After three or four little Motorola headpieces, I had made something that worked. It proved the concept. Then I took that to my prototyping friends, again worked through the process of refining the elements to the point of precision. Once there were no more questions to ask, I was done!

Fast forward two years: what I had thought was an idea became an award-winning magic trick. It was one of the most powerful magic tricks of my career and something that had never been done before. A truly original creation, manifested into reality by a spark of a thought that I could have let slip by me, but didn't. I was receiving encouragement from the world all around me to pursue what I loved, so I listened to myself, my gut, and everything else I could allow to flow through me.

So these are the two main creative processes I use. Either I research and develop my idea from mind maps, starting with basically nothing, or I know exactly what I want the trick or outcome to be and what to solve to make it happen. These are really just different starting points on a creative timeline. Sometimes the idea hits you over the head, and sometimes you slowly unearth it. Either way, you nurture your idea. There are merely different ways of nurturing, specific to each idea!

Any time that I research a project, product, or creative endeavor, I follow my interests. I am a huge techie, so I frequent sites like Kickstarter, Etsy, and YouTube to see newly released gadgets and toys. These are my go-to list of sites that I always scan through until something catches my eye.

Whether it's something that immediately appeals to my interests, or something so different and extravagant that it cannot be ignored, I play with it, push it around in my mind, and many times even buy it to dissect and analyze. As I scroll through these reference sites, I jot down any thoughts or ideas that come to mind. Once again, writing is my most essential tool, recording and acknowledging thoughts as they arise.

When it came to my latest invention called Fiddlestick, I recognized the market for what it was, and then wondered how I could change it for the better. Kickstarter, Etsy, Thingiverse… these sites are where it's all happening. These visual platforms bring a new sense of understanding to my own ideas, and help me to further pare down my options. I find products similar to my own idea, and study how others are fabricating, marketing, and packaging theirs. The nice thing about crowd funding websites like these is you get real time data on how well an item is selling and to what demographics.

I noticed that on Kickstarter a fidget toy called Fidget Cube made over 6 million dollars in less than 30 days. This was my spark for Fiddlestick. The next few months I bought every fidget toy on the planet. Played with them, tore them apart and decided what I liked best about them and what I hated. I pieced together some ideas and very rough 3D print and by accident the 3D file was corrupt and it left a big gap in the middle of my design. I played with this error for a while and decided to stick a small loop in the gap.

BOOM! I instantly knew a had something

good. This little loop allowed the Fiddlestick to spin around your finger in such a way that it became immediately addicting. I was able to take all the elements I loved from existing fidget toys and combined them into a sleek pen like toy that would fit into your pocket and be impossible to put down. I added a detachable LED spinner to go on the end and perfected the loop. The final product is something between a Bruce Lee nun-chuck and a futuristic fidget toy. You have to see it in action for yourself to truly understand.

I would love to write about how big of a success Fiddlestick was for me and that it allowed me to buy my dream house, car and boat. But the reality is the final units of Fiddlestick are being made as I write this. I am currently one month away from launching it onto Kickstarter. By the time you're reading this the "product launch Gods" will have spoken and together we can see if it was a dud or stud product. My fingers are crossed!

No matter what your creative pull, you should be able to find websites that streamline and support your niche. Find them and see what's out there!

After I've gathered a sufficient amount of information through this process, I review and streamline my notes. Anything that sticks out to me as I read through is set aside and rewritten, almost like a first edit of a manuscript. This more refined mind map then becomes my reference point for any further developments.

From here, I edit and work with my ideas until they are ready for further development. Now, out of the mind, into the physical. Actionable steps are next. I generally use a site like Fiverr, and request someone to build me a model for a small fee. However, you must ensure that those you work with are trustworthy. Don't overlook the importance of this if your creative project would be considered an intellectual property. And protect your ideas with non-disclosure agreements. Others will not be looking out for your best interests; they will be looking out for their own. You must take care of your creation and protect it!

In a nutshell, here is my process: I find out what I most enjoy in my niche or field of choice, I study that product and research others like it, I write mind maps and lists of the positives and negatives I see in the products already out there, and then I whittle down from here, until I'm ready to apply my findings to a goal timeline, and listing actionable steps I have to take to reach that goal.

In working with Pyro, I applied a very traditional research and development process to find and work through my idea to completion. With Decibel, I saw the end goal, but had no means to get there. I had to work the process backwards until I found the starting point. Once I had that starting point, the real work of joyful, playful dedication became of the utmost importance.

It really doesn't matter which process you use, so long as you continue to remain open to going wherever it takes you!

REALIZING MAGIC

What I love the most about a really good magic trick is how there is: a moment of wonder, astonishment and raw emotion for the person watching it. This moment can be present when a great song hits your ears for the first time, or when you hear such a passionately delivered speech that the hairs on the back of your neck stick up. Moments like these are what I cherish; where I find value, truth, discovery, surprise, and magic … where I find life.

These are the moments that have the power to take you away from every problem, concern, email, job prospect, or little annoyance that the world throws your way. They take us to a place where we can silence the madness around us and just exist within a state of magical wonder. Children wonder every second of every day, asking millions of questions and creating nonstop. I believe that, just like a good magic trick, your own creativity can bring you to this same moment of alluring escape and wonder.

The next part of this book will teach you the things to practice, recognize, and maintain in order to be the most creative person that you can be, and in order to let your inner creative voice sing out! When we have all died, the one thing that will remain is what we have chosen to create in this life. Let's try to focus on creating things that leave this world a little better off than it was when we got here, shall we?

The text following this page is your 30-Day Creativy Challenge. I recomend to first, flip the book over, and read Part 2.

Once you have read Part 2, come back and dive in head first!

DAY 1

DEFINE CREATIVITY FOR YOURSELF

Creativity can be found everywhere. You can be creative in absolutely everything you do. Think about it—you can be original in:

- **Dressing**

- **Cooking**

- **Drawing**

- **Writing**

- **Dancing**

- **Creating business ideas**

- **Raising children**

- **Building relationships**

The only limit to ingenuity are the boundaries you generate around it. Being creative is a conscious decision.

CREATIVE EXERCISE

An astonishing thing about everyone is that no two people are the same. We are, therefore, also creative in different ways! Life would have been quite boring if creativity were standardized and confined within certain parameters.

In thirty minutes, write down a list of twenty-five areas in which you can be creative.

Be specific! Here are a few examples:

- **Dress in my own way, not confirming to the norm.**

- **Find new ways to serve breakfast, or new dishes to eat in the morning.**

- **Remember friends' birthdays, and do something special and free for that occasion.**

- **Begin a picture journal.**

Now, do yours!

INTENTION OF THE ACTIVITY

*D*efine YOUR creativity. Who are you, and what makes your heart race faster? It is easy to be creative when doing the things you love. Identify areas of your life where you can be more creative.

MORE CREATIVITY TRIGGERS:

*P*ick something from your list and decide to do something with it today. Go back to this list from time to time and add more of it to your life. Make a conscious decision to start living more creatively!

free play space

DAY 2

PREPARE TO BE CREATIVE

*I*t is always easy to dream and make lists. What separates the dreamers from the doers is that doers will start finding ways to make their dreams a reality. Surrounding yourself with the tools of the trade—whether new or old—aids creativity. Also, if you've got a plan, you can execute it.

CREATIVE EXERCISE

*P*ick an area in which you want to be more creative from your list in the previous exercise. Write down five things that you can do to prepare. What would help you get energized enough to get started?

Let's say I want to be more creative in making breakfast. Here are five strategies to achieve this:

• **Buy new spatula.**

• **Sort out breakfast plates, tableware, and crockery. How would I present my breakfast in a creative way?**

• **I want to make something other than eggs! Find unconventional breakfast recipes that will be interesting, but still feel like breakfast to my guests or family, perhaps through an internet search.**

• **Try recipes beforehand, or pick a theme.**

• **Invite four friends for breakfast a week from today.**

INTENTION OF THE ACTIVITY

*F*ollow up on your creativity list. Don't let it stay in the planning stage, but do something constructive to make it a reality.

free play space

37

free play space

38

DAY 3

FINGERPRINTS

Your fingerprints have been with you since before you were born. Formed seven months after conception, they are a unique mishmash of ridges that make patterns of loops, whirls, arches, and dots, and leave behind marks on everything you touch. In 80 years of fingerprinting, no two sets have been found that matched each other.

CREATIVE EXERCISE

Let's think in a different way about fingerprints. Spend a few minutes considering the following ideas:

What if fingerprints did not have lines and squiggles, but other patterns, or even pictures? How would your ideal fingerprint look? If you would like to draw it, do so.

Now, imagine fingerprints could be seen. Where will you leave your fingerprint (with its unique pattern) today? Where would you like to leave your fingerprints?

How would your workplace or home look with your visible fingerprints everywhere? What would you do differently if others could see your fingerprints?

"Adermatoglyphia" is a disease where people are born without fingerprints. It is exceedingly rare, affecting only four known extended families worldwide. What would you do if you didn't have fingerprints? Can you use it to your advantage?

Does this exercise spark a creative idea for you? For example, think of a story about a boy intentionally leaving his fingerprints everywhere so his mom could see them.

INTENTION OF THE ACTIVITY

Seeing things in your own way!

MORE CREATIVITY TRIGGERS!

The fingerprints of koalas are so similar to humans that even experts have trouble telling them apart.

A 73-year-old woman bought a painting from a thrift store for $5 only to later discover that, thanks to a fingerprint on the canvas, it was actually an unsigned Jackson Pollock worth millions of dollars.

free play space

DAY 4

DRAW A WORD

A creative person can see common things in new ways, and are not hampered by physical constraints. They have the ability to ask: "Why not?"

CREATIVE EXERCISE

*T*his exercise is not original and has been around for a long time, but it will really get your creative juices flowing!

1. Set the timer on your phone for two minutes.

2. Now draw the following words, taking two minutes per word.

- **Flashy**

- **Dog**

- **Bounce**

The only criterion is that that you must use the physical letters of the word in order to create your drawing. You can use all the letters, or just one. It is not easy, but try to be as creative as you can!

Here is an example:

sm;)e

INTENTION OF THE ACTIVITY

*S*ee beyond what is in front of you. Develop creative thinking and seeing more—this concept can be used in design, creative writing, and even developing new products to trigger new ideas.

MORE CREATIVITY TRIGGERS:

free play space

free play space

42

DAY 5

FIND YOUR WORDS

*B*rainstorming is a very useful creative exercise. Usually, these ideas, even the silliest ones, can spark something creative in you. It is important not to hold back, but to write down everything that comes to mind.

CREATIVE EXERCISE

*O*ur exercise today comes in three parts:

Part 1: Grab any book, magazine, or pamphlet that is nearby. Don't go and look for a book; part of the challenge is to use what you already have.

Page through your book or magazine. You have five minutes to write down three words or phrases that jump out at you. Your focus must be to write down words or phrases that are new to you, or words you think can be used creatively. The words must resonate with you.

I used an Avon booklet. The words I found were "style—changing;" "orange you happy," and "feathering."

Part 2: The second part of today's challenge is to brainstorm about your words. Write down anything that comes to mind, no matter how silly.

Here's my list:

**Style-changing — Why change your style? What would trigger it? Would you change from drab to flashy, or from flashy to drab?
Story idea: superheroes.**

Orange you happy? — How can I use orange to make someone happy? Fruit and color. Oranges smell good; the smell can make me happy. Flashlight on my forehead, orange signals "happy?" A world where if you dress in orange, it signals happiness

Feathering — A little bird in a nest, without feathers. His feathers are growing, and it comes out black and stick-like. It itches. How would this little bird feel? Feather duvet in winter Eyelash-kisses = feathering

Part 3: Now, choose the brainstorming idea that you like the most. What are you going to do with it?

My end-result is a story idea about happy people wearing orange in a monotonous, colorless world. Orange is the only color, and only happiness matters. But how do they acquire happiness? (There's some more brainstorming needed, but I am thinking there must be a twist in all of this.)

INTENTION OF THE ACTIVITY

Creativity can be sparked in a number of ways. Brainstorming is an easy way to connect ideas. The intention of this activity was to showcase a method of starting the brainstorming process.

MORE CREATIVITY TRIGGERS!

More wonderful words:

Snuggery — a cozy little room

Eyesome — easy on the eyes. Attractive. Said of maidens and majestic views.

Badmash — an Indian hooligan

Kinnikinnick — a substance consisting of leaves and bark, smoked by the North American Indians

Bindlestiff — a tramp

Lobola — an African tradition where money or cattle is given by the bridegroom's family to "buy" the bride

Ciliad — a thousand things or a thousand years

DAY 6

DR. SEUSS

Theodor Seuss Geisel was a German-American author who wrote several of the most popular children's books of all time, selling over 600 million copies and being translated into more than twenty languages by the time of his death. Better known as "Dr. Seuss," he wrote classics like If I Ran the Zoo (1950), Horton Hears a Who! (1955), and The Cat in the Hat (1957).

Seuss wrote books that make people think and imagine. In On Beyond Zebra!, he invented an entirely new alphabet because, as the book's narrator explains, "In the places I go there are things that I see / That I never could spell if I stopped with the Z. / I'm telling you this 'cause you're one of my friends. / My alphabet starts where your alphabet ends."

CREATIVE EXERCISE

Spend forty-five minutes inventing you own alphabet beyond Z. Don't worry about being right or wrong—just be creative! You can draw symbols or make up words and letters. When you're finished, you can go and have a look at what Dr. Seuss came up with.

As always, go back to your creation and ask yourself: "Is there something more that I can do with this? How can I build on this idea?"

INTENTION OF THE ACTIVITY

Thinking outside the box and coming up with creative ideas. More brainstorming!

MORE CREATIVITY TRIGGERS

People often asked Dr. Seuss where he got his ideas. Since Seuss wasn't sure himself, he tended to invent answers. As he told one such questioner:

"This is the most asked question of any successful author. Most authors will not disclose their source for fear that other, less successful authors will chisel in on their territory. However, I am willing to take that chance. I get all my ideas in Switzerland, near the Forka Pass. There is a little town called Gletch, and two thousand feet up above Gletch there is a smaller hamlet called Uber Gletch. I go

45

there on the fourth of August every summer to get my cuckoo clock repaired. While the cuckoo is in the hospital, I wander around and talk to the people in the streets. They are very strange people, and I get my ideas from them." (http://m.seussville.com/biography.html)

free play space

DAY 7

CHEESE CHALLENGE

Cheese types are grouped or classified according to criteria such as length of aging, texture, methods of making, fat content, animal milk, country or region of origin, etc. Nobody is sure how many types of cheeses there are, as there is no universal method of classification. Yet, it is sufficient to say that there may be between 500-800 types of cheese in the world today.

CREATIVE EXERCISE

How many types of cheese have you tried? For today's challenge, you'll have to go to a supermarket or a deli. You can do some research beforehand and read up about different types of cheeses and what to eat with them.

Go and find a cheese that you've never had. Be bold! Try something that you would not normally choose. Gruyere, Roquefort, Camembert, or Ricotta? Gorgonzola, Stilton, Goat's Cheese, Brie, or Cheddar?

Invite a friend, open a bottle of wine, and try your cheese. Do you like it?

INTENTION OF THE ACTIVITY

Creativity can be found in trying new things. A true creative person should be willing to do something they haven't done before to broaden their horizons.

MORE CREATIVITY TRIGGERS!

So, you did not like the cheese you chose. What to do now? Think about ways to dispose of your cheese or how to use it in a different way.

Can you try it grilled?

Make a nice platter with biscuits and present it to your neighbors.

Would my dog eat cheese?

free play space

free play space

48

DAY 8

DESIGN YOUR DREAM HOUSE

*M*y dream house is a house by the sea. It sits high on a cliff and looks out over the endless ocean. I don't need much: a view, a thousand books, and a coffee machine! I want a cozy bedroom, a fireplace, and somewhere to entertain friends.

CREATIVE EXERCISE

*D*esign your own dream house today. The idea is not to draw something up to scale, but rather to do it as a doodle. Include everything that is essential to you.

INTENTION OF THE ACTIVITY

*C*reative thinking and having fun! We might not all, have our dream homes just yet. But that sure as hell, doesn't mean we can't imagine one up for the time being.

MORE CREATIVITY TRIGGERS!

*D*o you want a creative space in your dream house? What would it look like? Is it possible to make this a reality?

free play space

49

DAY 9

BEAUTIFUL DOLLS

In the African language of Zulu, Ntomben-tle means "beautiful girl." Molemo Kgomo, a South African mom, designed a doll range after identifying the lack of pretty black dolls in the market in which her daughter could relate. In doing so, she discovered a niche. It turned out that many more African moms wanted dolls that represent their own cultures.

The Ntombenhle range represents a variety of African dolls true to different African countries. Unlike typical Barbie type dolls, the Ntombentle dolls have a fuller figure, curlier hair, and bigger eyes. They are also dressed in colorful traditional African outfits, representing the Ndebele, Sotho, Xhosa, Zulu, Tsonga, Xhosa, Pedi, and Venda cultures.

http://ntombenhledolls.co.za/

CREATIVE EXERCISE

Design a doll for someone in your family. How would a doll that represents your culture and your family values look? Think about the morals you want to convey. In what clothes would you dress your doll? Take as long as you like on this exercise.

INTENTION OF THE ACTIVITY

Thinking outside the box and designing to fulfill a specific need. Creativity can be sparked by a need.

MORE CREATIVITY TRIGGERS

Use this activity to engage a child. Let her (or him!) design a doll. Afterwards, try and make the doll out of paper maché, or even material.

free play space

free play space

51

DAY 10

COFFEE, ANYONE?

Coffee is everywhere these days. We brew it in our kitchens in fancy machines or go to our favorite outlet to get our preferred fix. Many restaurants serve a quality cup made with better beans.

CREATIVE EXERCISE

You want to open up a coffee shop. What would you do to capitalize on the coffee trend? How will you get people to come to your coffee shop, rather than the next one?

Remember, competition is brutal. Try and be as creative as possible. Give yourself twenty-five minutes to brainstorm and come up with five original ideas. Combine coffee with anything, and see what you can come up with.

INTENTION OF THE ACTIVITY

Creative thinking and idea development.

MORE CREATIVITY TRIGGERS!

Combine coffee with cats! Meow Parlor is the first permanent cat café in New York. Inspired by cat cafés of Japan, this unique café puts you in the company of cats. Each of the cats is available for adoption. There is even an owl café popping up in London with proceeds being given to charity.

Forty Ninth Parallel in Vancouver serves espresso with freshly baked doughnuts as you sit at the bar.

free play space

free play space

DAY 11

BUCKET LIST

*T*hese days, everyone knows about bucket lists. It is a list of things you write down and promise yourself to do before you die.

Zackham had created his own list called "Justin's List of Things to Do before I Kick the Bucket." The first item on his list was to have a screenplay produced at a major Hollywood studio. After a while, it occurred to him that the notion of a "bucket list" could itself be an idea for a film, so he wrote a screenplay about two dying men racing to complete their own bucket lists with the time they had left.

(https://en.wiktionary.org/wiki/bucket_list)

CREATIVE EXERCISE

*B*egin your own bucket list. This is not an exercise to do quickly, so there is no time limit. Rather, promise yourself that you are really going to think about it: if I died today, what would I regret not doing?

Write the list down in your notebook and keep adding to it. Start with naming your list "Designing My Own Life: Ten Things to Do Before I Die." For some people, ten goals would be enough, while others might find the list growing to fifty items.

Just remember, making a list accomplishes nothing. You must also be willing to do something about it. Be critical—are my goals realistic? How am I going to achieve the items on my list?

It need not be expensive or hard to do. Just think about what YOU really would like to do or experience before you die.

INTENTION OF THE ACTIVITY

*T*ime is short. If you want to be creative or accomplish more in life, plan for it.

MORE CREATIVITY TRIGGERS!

Some bucket list ideas:

- **Wrap a snake around your neck.**

- **Ride an elephant.**

- **Sleep in a haystack.**

- **Find your high school best friend.**

- **Camp on a beach.**

- **Be in the front row of a concert.**

- **Partake in a food fight.**

- **Drink tea in a tree house.**

- **Learn to crochet.**

free play space

DAY 12

MUG

*W*e think we need to do big, complicated things in order to be creative. Sometimes the best ideas are simple—just look at the world differently.

CREATIVE EXERCISE

*T*oday, you are going to design your own coffee mug. The idea is to create the coffee mug you've always wanted. Choose the color, the material, the shape. If you already have a favorite mug, think about how you can improve on it. Can you design a lid for it so that you can take it with you? You can take as long on this exercise as you wish.

1. Think for a few minutes about the material you would like to use. Paper, clay, Play-Doh, wood, or recycled items?

2. You can simply design the mug, or you can actually try and make it.

3. Think about how and where YOU drink coffee. The mug must be personalized just for you.

4. Is the mug plain? Or does it have a picture or writing on it?

Finished? Consider getting your mug made just for you—or perhaps there's a business idea lurking here.

INTENTION OF THE ACTIVITY

*C*reative thinking and idea development.

MORE CREATIVITY TRIGGERS

free play space

free play space

57

DAY 13

THE CREATIVE FRIEND

I find that being a creative friend brings me lots of pleasure. Surprising my friends with creativeness is one of my core goals in life. All it requires is a bit of listening, a bit of thinking, and a bit of planning. The main rationale of being a creative friend is not to do it to get recognition. I do it to add fun to a relationship, and to make someone feel really special. What can be more rewarding than to know that someone spent time thinking about you and planning something that would really speak to you as a person?

CREATIVE EXERCISE

Do something creative for a friend today. You don't have to spend money. Really think about your friend. What do you know about the person that you can use? Make a list of the things the person likes to do. What would thrill your friend? It could be as small as an offer of babysitting for two hours so that she could go out for a while.

You can do this as a random act of kindness, or as part of planning for a special occasion.

INTENTION OF THE ACTIVITY

Creativeness can be found in all of life. You can be creative in planning an event (or a gift) and executing it.

MORE CREATIVITY TRIGGERS

I have a friend who loves owls. She even raised two of them. One year, I surprised her with a birthday package full of owl things. It contained an owl notebook, owl fridge magnets, and a little owl handbag.

I like asking friends about their favorite types of presents. You'll be surprised by the answers you'll get. Some friends really like everyday things such as chocolates and bath oils. Some hate them! Everyone has different tastes. Remember what they are, and use them.

free play space

DAY 14

SAY IT WITH CHOCOLATE

*I*t is surprisingly easy to make your own chocolate. If you experiment a bit, you might be able to find the perfect consistency and sweetness. Be creative with your homemade chocolate!

CREATIVE EXERCISE

*I*f you don't like this recipe, there are lots more to be found on the Internet. Use this one or find another, but make your own chocolate today.

Here's what you'll need:

- **1/2 cup virgin coconut oil**

- **1/2 cup (raw) organic cocoa powder**

- **Choose one: Organic honey, stevia, or raw cane sugar (to taste)**

METHOD

*G*ently heat the coconut oil for 1 minute. Mix in the cocoa powder until you get a smooth consistency. Add the honey, sweetener, or sugar to taste.

Pour the melted chocolate on a pan/plate/ice cube tray.

Place in the refrigerator to set for 45 minutes.

Enjoy!

INTENTION OF THE ACTIVITY

*Y*ou can be creative in lots of ways. Cooking/making chocolate is one of them!

MORE CREATIVITY TRIGGERS

*Y*ou can jazz up your chocolate with:

- **cocoa nibs or chocolate chips**

- **dried berries**

- **raisins**

- -- chopped dates

- -- crushed nuts, almonds, or seeds

- chili powder

- green tea extract

- carob

- anything else you like!

free play space

DAY 15

NAPKIN NOTES

*G*arth Callaghan learned he had kidney cancer shortly after his daughter, Emma, turned twelve. Resolved to make the time he had left significant, he made a promise to compile years' worth of notes to give his daughter through to her high school graduation. He started by putting these notes in her lunch box, but also stockpiled notes, just in case. His mission is to spread the word about connecting, in a meaningful and thoughtful manner. (http://www.napkinnotesdad.com)

CREATIVE EXERCISE

*T*hink about Garth's mission. Does it ignite something in you? Is there someone you would like to write a note to? You can plan a series of notes, or just one. The important thing is to think about connecting to someone in an original manner. Take fifteen minutes to think and to plan, then write your notes.

INTENTION OF THE ACTIVITY

*T*o be creative on a deeper level. Leave behind a legacy.

MORE CREATIVITY TRIGGERS

*W*rite some notes leading up to an event such as a birthday, anniversary, or wedding. Write notes to your grandchildren or children, and save them to be found later. Leave anonymous notes to encourage someone.

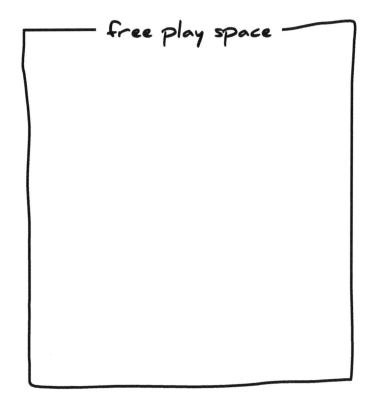

free play space

DAY 16

SUPERHEROES

*A*ccording to the Merriam-Webster dictionary, a superhero is "a fictional hero having extraordinary or superhuman powers; also: an exceptionally skillful or successful person."

Some long-running superheroes are: Batman, Spider-Man, Superman, Captain America, Wonder Woman, Iron Man, the Flash, Wolverine, Green Lantern, and Hulk. (https://en.wikipedia.org/wiki/Superhero)

CREATIVE EXERCISE

*O*vernight, you've turned into a superhero! The only problem is that you don't know yet what your super powers will be. All you know is that your power is connected to your initials. So, what could it be?

1. Write down your initials.

2. Your superpower is hiding in these letters.

3. Take fifteen minutes and write down anything that could be hidden in your initials.

4. Find your superpower! Write it down.

For example, my initials are A.W. I could be an Awesome Wanderer, an Airborne Welcome, or an Automatic Weeper.

As an Airborne Welcome, my superpower is to welcome visitors to my home from the air. I swoop down and, with dramatic flair, guide them inside. I am the Airborne Welcome!

INTENTION OF THE ACTIVITY

*C*reative thinking, generation of ideas. What can you do with the superhero you've created?

MORE CREATIVITY TRIGGERS

- **More superpowers:**

- **Body Part Substitution**

- **Duplication**

- Invisibility

- Immobility

- Bone Protrusion

- Helicopter Propulsion

- Cyclone Spinning

- Fat Manipulation

- Bubble Generation

- Stench Generation

- Nerve-Gas Emission

- Sonic Scream

- Hyper Breath

free play space

DAY 17

THE MEMORY CASTLE

A Memory Castle is an imaginary place that you create for yourself. The idea is to store mnemonic images here. The most common type of Memory Castle involves making a journey through a place you know well, like a building or town. Along that journey, there are specific locations that you always visit in the same order. The Memory Castle is a tool to help you remember specific information: names, numbers, or a speech. It can also be used as a study aid.

CREATIVE EXERCISE

Take some time to read about Memory Castles on the Internet. Here are some links:
https://www.wikihow.com/Build-a-Memory-Palace
https://litemind.com/memory-palace/

Now, build your own Memory Castle to remember something you always forget. It can be your social security number, a telephone number, or even your shopping list. It's great fun!

INTENTION OF THE ACTIVITY

A new way of being creative; thinking differently about remembering things. The Memory Castle is also a useful tool for students.

MORE CREATIVITY TRIGGERS

*S*huffle a deck of playing cards and try memorizing the order. Think of the magic tricks you could accomplish.

free play space

DAY 18

CREATIVE DAYS

*P*i (Greek letter "ϖ") is the symbol used in mathematics to represent a constant, the ratio of the circumference of a circle to its diameter, which is approximately 3.14159.

CREATIVE EXERCISE

*P*i Day is celebrated on March 14th (3/14) around the world.

Today, you must create three celebration days for normal things. You can use the date as a trigger (as with Pi Day), or you can just think about anything you believe needs its own day. You can create a day especially for your own family to celebrate, or you can think in the wider context.

Write down three ideas. Are there some ideas here that you could use for fundraising? If you've thought about a special family day, try and implement it.

INTENTION OF THE ACTIVITY

*C*reative thinking, living mindfully, fundraising ideas.

MORE CREATIVITY TRIGGERS

• **November 12th is International Tongue Twister day.**

• **International Underlings day is on leap year day each year. The next one will be on the 29th of February, 2020.**

• **International Tuba day is on the first Friday in May each year.**

free play space

66

free play space

DAY 19

THE PROBING CREATOR

*T*he creative person has an inquisitive mind. He wants to know about an array of things: business ideas, weird animals, ancient history, and current manufacturing techniques. You never know when some of these concepts will come together to form a new idea. It might take six minutes or six years, but somewhere down the line, there is always the possibility of an "aha" moment.

CREATIVE EXERCISE

*S*pend thirty minutes surfing the Internet. Start with searching 'weird and strange animals,' and let the search lead you to other things. Randomly click on anything that interests you. Write down ideas as they come to you. The goal is to end with ten ideas in your notebook that inspire you.

Can you connect some of these ideas in a way? Perhaps it would be a good idea to set a timer for this exercise; you might spend more time on it than you were prepared to!

INTENTION OF THE ACTIVITY

*U*nderstand that creativeness is a process, and sometimes you need to support the process with creativity triggers. Also, two random ideas that connect can form a whole new idea.

MORE CREATIVITY TRIGGERS

*K*ickstarter and ThinkCad are gold mines of abstract ideas.

http://descriptivewords.org/descriptive-words-for-ocean/

free play space

DAY 20

THE CREATIVE DANCER

*T*oday, we will take creativeness to a new level! Einstein called dancers "the athletes of God." Let's dance!

CREATIVE EXERCISE

*C*reate a dance that is a fit to Albert's words. Dance for laughter, dance for tears! You might feel more comfortable doing it when no one can see you.

You can make your dance as extensive or as short as you want, but it must embody all the words above: You must show laughter, tears, madness, etc. Be sure to create the dream at the end.

Dance your dance more than once. Write down in your notebook, if you wish, how you felt while creating it and how it felt to dance it out.

INTENTION OF THE ACTIVITY

*B*e creative while dancing! The emotions can be very powerful, and will definitely free your spirit!

MORE CREATIVITY TRIGGERS

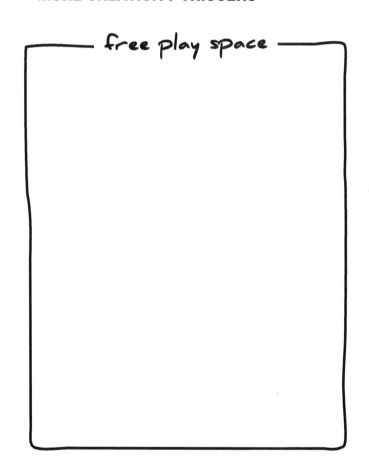
free play space

DAY 21

WHAT TO DO WITH MY CELL PHONE?

*I*f aliens were to look down at us, they might think that we humans are programmed in every move we make by a palm-sized slab of glass. It has become a cold fact: we can no longer live off the grid. Everything we do is directly determined by devices that are always at our sides.

CREATIVE EXERCISE

*T*oday's exercise comes in two parts:

1. Use five minutes to think about what you can do to live a more meaningful life. Do you want your children and grandchildren to remember you as someone who'd rather look at their phone than look them in the eye? How can you use your cell phone less?

2. Research how you can use your cell phone to be more creative. There has to be some good in it too, right? The Internet is full of articles, but here are a few ideas:

- Leave an old phone in the kitchen on which to store all your recipes.

- Heavy and expensive textbooks can be downloaded and carried around on your phone.

- You can train your dog (or even your cat) with special apps.

- Create a scavenger hunt. Participants must take photos with their phones to record the evidence as they find it.

- Using the recorder on your phone, record a personal log each day. Start with the words "Today, I…"

- Use an old phone as a digital photo frame. Flash inspirational quotes on it.

- Play music or make videos on your phone.

INTENTION OF THE ACTIVITY

*C*ell phones can be useful and help you to find access to more creative ideas, but they can also squash your creativity. The answer lies in finding the balance.

MORE CREATIVITY TRIGGERS!

*L*ook around you today. Try and count how many people are with someone else, but not talking or sharing the moment. Instead, they are looking at their phones.

Use an old phone to make a wallet:

DAY 22

QUICK ILLUSTRATIONS

*W*e each have different talents, and although not all of us think we are artistic when creating illustrations, it is a useful tool to unlock creativity and potential ideas. If you've got a problem you can't solve, try drawing. Just let your mind wander, and draw out the different aspects of the problem. Perhaps you'll see it in a new light afterwards.

CREATIVE EXERCISE

*D*ivide a blank piece of paper into eight blocks. Quickly write down the first eight words or phrases you can think of that relate to your problem. An example follows:

Your problem is to find time to be creative.

The words I came up with were:

1. A Clock

2. All the other things stealing time

3. Little me, torn

4. Where can I find time? Ideas?

5. In what can I be creative?

6. Creative space?

7. How big is the problem?

8. Peace and creativity

Going through the blocks one by one, quickly draw the image you conjure up when you think about the word. Draw it any way you like, whether realistic or more like a doodle. Don't spend too much time on each drawing. The idea is to pen down the first image that comes to mind.

Show your little drawings to someone and explain why you saw each object or idea the way you did. Did you get a new solution to your problem?

INTENTION OF THE ACTIVITY

*Y*ou may not be an artist, but all of us are creative in our drawings! The intention of this activity is to simply be creative and find answers in our subconscious. Solutions can come to you in the weirdest forms.

MORE CREATIVITY TRIGGERS!

*C*hildren love to play this game. Divide the page in eight blocks and suggest topics for the blocks one by one. Ask them to draw a cat, then a coffee mug. Next, they must draw love, then sunshine.

Compare drawings after each block is finished. It is great to see how each child interprets the topics by using his imagination.

free play space

free play space

74

DAY 23

PHOBIAS

*T*here are literally hundreds of phobias. Formal phobias have been created for absolutely anything of which anyone could possibly be afraid. Some of the most common phobias are:

- "Acrophobia," which is the fear of heights,

- "Arachnophobia," the fear of spiders, and

- "Ophidiophobia," the fear of snakes

CREATIVE EXERCISE

*T*he following are three phobias. What are these people afraid of? Write down five ideas for each phobia. The answers are below. Don't peek! The intention of the exercise is for you to do some creative brainstorming.

- **Ablutophobia**

- **Catoptrophobia**

- **Liticaphobia**

*N*ow, for the second half of the exercise: What are you most afraid of? Think up a name for your own phobia and use it in conversations. Why not? You are, after all, a creative person.

INTENTION OF THE ACTIVITY

*T*hinking outside of the box, creative brainstorming.

MORE CREATIVITY TRIGGERS

Ablutophobia – Fear of bathing.

Catoptrophobia – Fear of mirrors.

Liticaphobia – Fear of lawsuits.

*P*eople suffering from Hippopotomonstrosesquippedaliophobia tend to experience a great deal of anxiety when faced with long words. It is indeed ironical that the scientific name given to this phobia is such a long one. (http://www.fearof.net)

free play space

DAY 24

LIFE LESSONS

*D*riving does not come naturally to me. I think it is because my head is in the clouds too much! Therefore, I've had my share of small car accidents in the twenty years I've been driving. I can truly say, however, that I've learned from each of these accidents. (I was fortunate that none of them were too serious.)

My scares have taught me much more than good advice could have.

CREATIVE EXERCISE

*T*hink about the lessons that life taught you. Can you make a list?

Write a letter or an email to somebody, telling them about your life lessons. Perhaps you've had enough lessons to inspire you to do something more with them. Begin a blog or think about writing your memoir.

Can't think of anything? Impossible!
Dig deeper!

INTENTION OF THE ACTIVITY

*I*nnovative writing, but also planting the idea that nothing goes to waste. Every occurrence in life means something, and you can learn from it. Use experiences as a catalyst to fuel creativity.

MORE CREATIVITY TRIGGERS

*T*here are countless biographies and memoirs that can be read about extraordinary life adventures and life lessons. If this is not your type of reading, just try it once. Choose any topic that interests you and look for a book about it.

There are books written about mountaineering, trail walking, abductions, and crimes. There are books that real doctors wrote about their training and experiences, and books about 9/11, dementia, and cancer. There are stories about drug abuse and anorexia, and real families that have struggled. Think of a topic and you will find a book on it. Read it and enrich your life.

— free play space —

78

DAY 25

YOUR CREATIVE ANIMAL

The pink fairy armadillo (Chlamyphorus truncatus), which is also known as the Pichiciego, is the smallest species of armadillo known. It is between 90-115 mm long, excluding its tail, and weighs less than a pound. This is the only species of armadillo that has its dorsal shell almost completely separate from its body.

This unique animal resides in the dry grasslands and sandy plains of central Argentina. This sandy environment works well for the pink fairy armadillo, since they are excellent diggers. In fact, they have the ability to completely bury themselves in a matter of seconds if threatened.

CREATIVE EXERCISE

Do you think the animal in the example above is real? Spend two minutes deciding, and give a reason.

Now, using the example as a basis, create your own animal. It must have a scientific name, and you must include how it looks, its habitat, and what it can do. Be as original (and believable) as possible.

Think about how you can use your animal in a creative way. You can use your animal as a main character in a story. You can tell the story or write it down. You can draw your animal. Or you can just have fun with the exercise, and leave it at that.

INTENTION OF THE ACTIVITY

Imaginative thinking. You can use existing facts to trigger creativity.

MORE CREATIVITY TRIGGERS!

There really are pink fairy armadillos! The extract above comes from a-z animals (https://a-z-animals.com/animals/pink-fairy-armadillo/).

More facts:

- **The pink fairy armadillo is one of the rarest animals in the world.**

- **They move through the sand as smoothly and fast as fish swim in the** sea. However, they are not able to walk on ground very comfortably.

• The armadillo has poor vision.

• Predators of pink fairy armadillos are wild boars, domestic dogs, and cats.

(http://animalstime.com/pink-fairy-armadillo-facts)

free play space

DAY 26

YOUR DOG IS THE ONLY THING THAT LOVES YOU MORE THAN YOURSELF

Do you have a dog? The natural intuition of dogs plays a big part in why they are called "man's best friends." While they may not be able to speak our language, dogs are empathetic, compassionate, and fierce protectors who get the message across clearly without words.

CREATIVE EXERCISE

Think about any pet you've had or an animal with which you've had contact. Can you recount a story where the animal has "spoken" to you? What was the message?

Spread a bit of creativeness to your pet today. Surprise it with a snack or an extra walk. Talk to your pet, but also make some time to "listen." What do you hear? Use this activity as a conversation starter with a friend or a child.

INTENTION OF THE ACTIVITY

Thinking more broadly to find inspiration!

MORE CREATIVITY TRIGGERS

Here are stories about two animals that actually talked. Read more at: http://edition.cnn.com/2010/LIVING/wayoflife/05/14/mf.animals.that.could.talk/index.html

Hoover the Seal: This seal often told people to "Get outta here!" or ask, "How are ya?" He could say his name and a few other phrases, all with a thick Bostonian accent.

Alex the Parrot: He could identify fifty different objects, knew seven colors and shapes, and recognized many different kinds of materials, including wool, paper, and wood.

free play space

81

free play space

82

DAY 27

WHAT IS IT REALLY?

There is no right or wrong when being creative! Some of the best ideas for businesses were born out of something going wrong.

CREATIVE EXERCISE

Spend a few minutes thinking about what is holding you back from being more creative. Is it the opinion of others? Are you too critical of your own work? Perhaps you think your work must be too perfect.

Make the resolution today that you will not be afraid anymore. Good things can come out of wrongs! Just make a resolution to DO, to create, and to find what your heart loves. Then, there is no limit to what you can do.

INTENTION OF THE ACTIVITY

Believe in yourself. Believe in the creative process.

MORE CREATIVITY TRIGGERS

Here are two inventions that were created out of mistakes:

Artificial sweetener: In 1879, after a long day of working with coal tar, chemist Constantin Fahlberg came home to have dinner with his wife without first washing his hands. While eating his meal, Fahlberg noticed everything he put in his mouth had a sweet taste, and discovered the saccharin on his hands was responsible.

Post-It Notes: In 1968, scientist Spencer Silver at the 3M company created a very weak adhesive that would peel off when removed from any surface. The funny thing was that he was, in fact, trying to create a super-strong adhesive. No one thought there was any use for such a product, until another scientist, Art Fry, realized that the little pieces of paper made great book marks for his church songs without leaving residue on the page.

(http://www.storypick.com/inventions-made-by-mistake)

free play space

84

DAY 28

DON'T BE SHY.

What if there was no Michelangelo or no Shakespeare?

The world would have been less creative, no question! Luckily, we don't know what we are missing, but wouldn't it be sad if the world were denied a great, resourceful, ingenious offering coming from you?

CREATIVE EXERCISE

Spend five minutes listing all your artistic strong points. What can you offer the world? Now, using twenty-five more minutes, expand on these offerings.

Here is a small example:

I have a great imagination.
I can write children's books where children can read about wildly ridiculous adventures.
I can organize parties with a twist.

I can enrich my own children's lives with memories, like creating my own alternative to the tooth fairy… the "Toe kisser." He will visit when you were especially sweet during the day, and leave a sticker on your big toe during the night.

INTENTION OF THE ACTIVITY

Exploring your unique way(s) of being creative. Do not conform to what everyone else is doing, but celebrate your own individuality.

MORE CREATIVITY TRIGGERS

- **How can you be different in:**

- **Cooking meals?**

- **Dancing?**

- **Planning your garden?**

- **Driving to work?**

free play space

86

DAY 29

SINGING IN THE SHOWER OF CREATIVITY

*W*e've talked throughout these activities about connecting two or three seemingly unrelated things to inspire creativity. Today's activity might seem silly, but try and really think about it as you do it. What did you feel? How could you use this feeling in another context?

CREATIVE EXERCISE

*C*hoose a song you know well. If you are not sure of all the words, quickly look them up and familiarize yourself with it again.

Now, sing it! Imagine you are in front of an audience and you must sing your song to the best of your ability.

Examine your feelings afterwards. Did you like to sing like that? If not, why not?

INTENTION OF THE ACTIVITY

*B*eing in touch with your inner self. What will make you "sing?"

MORE CREATIVITY TRIGGERS

*I*n the wildly successful series Frasier, Frasier once had to write a theme song for his radio show. In the end, his dad came up with the winning idea, a simple but catchy tune:

- **What's new? I'm listenin'**

- **Feelin' blue? I'm listenin'…**

- **Feelin' sad, feelin' mad, feelin' glad, feelin' bad**

- **I'm listenin'!**

(http://www.kacl780.net/frasier/transcripts/season_7/episode_13/theyre_playing_our_song.html)

Have you ever thought about writing your own theme song? It can be silly or serious.

free play space

88

DAY 30

INTRODUCTION

You've worked through twenty-nine of these exercises! I really hope you are more in touch with your creative side. It is important not to let it go to waste. Deliberately try and be more original every day!

Ask yourself in any situation: Is there a creative way to do this? Is there more than one way to do it? How can I do it differently? And remember, you are living resourcefully only to please yourself—to be a better person and to find pleasure in everyday life.

CREATIVE EXERCISE

You've been commissioned to supply me with three creative ideas to include in my next book. Did some of these creative exercises make you think of something you would like to present to me? Do you have your own idea about creativity?

Use forty-five minutes to write down your ideas. What can one do to live more imaginatively? Would you have liked other types of creative ideas in this book? Write it down in your notebook and add it to your repertoire!

INTENTION OF THE ACTIVITY

The beauty of being creative is that all of us are different, and someone else might add a whole new perspective on how we see creativity!

MORE CREATIVITY TRIGGERS

Take these ideas and start writing your book. Write everything you think, fell and question about this beautiful mystery called creativity.

free play space

89

free play space

90

CPSIA information can be obtained
at www.ICGtesting.com
Printed in the USA
LVHW071653220419
615086LV00021B/1468/P

This book is split into two sections as you will see from flipping
through the pages. Part one is the story of how creativity helped
save my life. Part 2 is the practical action steps you can use daily to find and nurture your own creative superhero. Just like this
book, the creative process has many angles, many sides, and
many surprises. My promise to you is this:

If you do the provided creativity challenge, as well the CREATE
morning routine, daily for 30 days, you will transform your life in
ways you could never have imagined.

My goal with this book is to share with you the tools and stories
I have used to find my inner creative superhero. Creativity truly did save my life and this book is my gratitude prayer to it. My
hope is that it adds value to your life and sparks a creative inferno
inside you that changes the way you look at the world around you.

Edited by Keira Faer
Cover Design by Adam Wilber
Layout and Graphic Design by Branden Wolf

Adam Wilber
2017

ADAM WILBER

inventor • keynote speaker • magician

CONTENTS

Magic Is…

Improve Your Creative Mindset:
- Confidence || Ritual
- Positivity || Humor
- Curiosity || Play

Navigate Environmental Factors:
- Combat Procrastination
- Take Risks
- Take Care Of Yourself

Innovate:
- Get Inspired
- Think Like A Child
- Read More

Actualize Your Magic:
- Brainstorm
- Visualize
- Finalize

MAGIC
The Creative Solution

"CREATIVITY IS JUST CONNECTING THINGS. WHEN YOU ASK CREATIVE PEOPLE HOW THEY DID SOMETHING, THEY FEEL A LITTLE GUILTY BECAUSE THEY DIDN'T REALLY DO IT, THEY JUST SAW SOMETHING. IT SEEMED OBVIOUS TO THEM AFTER A WHILE."

– Steve Jobs

*M*agic is ... everywhere around us. This universe of ours is a big, magical, and often scary place. When we take a minute to reflect on it, we recognize how our existence is magic, in and of itself. We are magic, and we are connected to all other magical elements. The sky is magic, in all its blue hues; the fish we find swimming in the river are magic in their upstream struggle. Mother Nature is filled with wonder, which is why it's surprising when we, the recipients of that wonder, fail to recognize it.

Sometimes life pulls us in directions we don't expect. We win some, we lose some, and after a particularly rotten struggle, we persevere to fight another day. Even if you don't have other dependents, you are your own dependent as an adult. And adulting can be just how it sounds: dull.

For individuals with dependents trying to do the right thing, there are long hours spent working to make ends meet. Finances have to be stretched to their utmost capacity, and at the end of each day, the body is fatigued and in desperate need of downtime.

Life can feel like a constant war zone, and we, the warriors without rest. The mindset so many of us hold onto is that there seem to be so many "serious" issues to handle every day, that there's no time to entertain more "frivolous" undertakings, such as creativity.

This is understandable on the surface. If looked at carefully, our inability to connect to the creative genius within us or to appreciate the full extent of its usefulness is why we live unhappy and under-fulfilled lives. We spend all our lives working, and even when the universe conspires in our favor by offering something tangible to show for all our hard work, there is a vacuum that can't be filled.

There is magic in all facets of life, just sitting there, waiting to be discovered. Why, then, do we search so assiduously for something that already exists within us?

You have your own fountain of magic, whoever you are and whatever your story might be. There is just one thing: unless you recog-

nize it and are able to showcase it in all its glory, the magic within you will just continue to sit there, static, a relic of years gone by and splendor forgotten.

This half of the book will supply you with practical, easily applicable ways of finding this magic, and incorporating it into your life. I see it functioning as a glossary or rule book for the creative process. Whereas, in the first section, you find the clear pathway or the clear ritual, in this section, you'll find yourself and your real struggles.

You will also find some golden nuggets of creative advice from individuals other than myself scattered throughout this section of the book. These essays and interviews were originally included in my first book, Creative Magic, and have emerged from some of the most creative minds in the magic community. I'm lucky enough to call these people friends, though I find myself inspired by their perspectives and creative integrity as though they were my mentors. I hope you take something meaningful from their ideas of what creativity means to them.

I know that some of my favorite books are the ones with captivating interruptions. It's always fun to read a book, and, along the way, find things to revisit at a later date. So be sure to enjoy your time spent navigating this treasure chest of creative goodies!

IMPROVE YOUR CREATIVE MINDSET

Keeping an open mind can be really tough. I have struggled with it quite a bit in my own life. Each of us is brought up with a certain set of beliefs and moral values that become second nature to us as we grow. Breaking free from these beliefs can pose a problem, up to the extent that it causes rifts between us and those in our lives once we attempt to challenge these beliefs. However, being open-minded can benefit us in all areas of our lives! Read on below to see how enlightening it can be.

FREEDOM

There is a certain sense of freedom that comes with keeping an open mind. Just recognizing and accepting ideologies that are different from your own is liberating. You are not shackled by self-imposed or societally imposed sets of values. Allow yourself to view life from different vantage points, not just a myopic point of view.

HONESTY

Open-mindedness and honesty are sort of a package deal. When you are consistently open-minded, you're no longer bound by the constraints of one single idea or plan: you can freely admit when you are wrong on certain issues. Every truth you know can be challenged. Knowing there is always more to something than meets the eye frees the mind.

RELINQUISHING CONTROL

Keeping an open mind affords you the opportunity to release. The space for examining new ideas opens up once you realize that you don't need to be fully in control of your thoughts at all times. You can challenge your current beliefs and re-examine your stance on many issues.

EXPERIENCING CHANGES

With open-mindedness comes the exposure to a new world and new experiences. You will allow yourself the space to change and to experience the full fluidity of that change. Once control is relinquished, changes occur naturally and unfold as needed.

STRENGTHENING YOURSELF

The strength and resilience of the mind define the perceived experience. Are you swayed by others' thoughts and opinions easily? An open mind helps not only to encourage acceptance, but also to encourage a sense of integrity and assurance in one's self.

A SELF-ESTEEM BOOST

When you keep an open mind, you begin to develop a strong sense of self. Your willingness to learn new things and question existing ideas increases your awareness of the world around you, helping you to gain clarity and insight into how it works, and assurance about the role you play in it.

INTROSPECTION

To sustain an open mind for the long haul, you will need to get in touch with your personal beliefs and values. Some quality time spent contemplating what you consider to be of the most (and least) importance in your life will benefit you greatly as you entertain new ideas and perspectives.

We don't define our values as a means of building a birdcage around ourselves, but rather as a means of encouraging stability and integrity as we funnel through alternative experiences. Read on below for some ways of encouraging true introspection:

CREATE A QUIET SPACE

Your quiet space depends on your personal preferences. It will not necessarily be a place for you to sit; it could be an activity or even a mindset. Your quiet place could be soaking in a bath, drinking a cup of coffee, or taking a walk down to the park. The most important thing is that it should be free from the distractions of others. You should be able to own that time as yours alone, so that you have the space to examine your thoughts without fear of judgment.

Once you have found your ideal spot, find a way to relax. Try to calm any anxieties or negative thoughts that arise. Perhaps, begin with a ritual or meditation or maybe even some movement or a yoga asana, to connect yourself wholly: mind, body, and spirit.

ASK QUESTIONS

*W*e learn by asking questions. We gain deeper insights and come up with more innovative solutions to better our world when we explore things. The best thinkers ask endless questions, as they know full well they will always find a solution somewhere along the way.

Begin to ask yourself questions that will scratch the surface of who you are, revealing what matters the most to you. Ask yourself, for example, what makes you feel the most like yourself: the most comfortable, the least anxious, and the happiest. Ask yourself what you feel your true purpose is and what role you play (or want to play) in society.

Cultivate the habit of paying attention to details and asking yourself questions as they arise. And even as you begin to question your way through the world, you may not always have the answers immediately. Don't rush yourself; keep asking the questions. The road to self-discovery is not one to be taken at top speed.

JOURNAL

*T*ake notes on what you discover, or, perhaps, free write the questions and answers as they arise. Some things will come into better focus while writing about them, helping you to see the important things more clearly. Also, what has been committed to paper can't be lost. As long as you don't lose the paper, of course...

Remember you are talking only to yourself while writing, so you don't have to worry about anybody else looking at or judging you. Allow yourself to be open and expressive. Write about how your day went, what made you sad, what made you happy, the people you met, and your perception of them. Just write whatever is on your mind. Empty it all out on the pages of your diary, and don't be afraid to write your greatest secrets or fears. You have no reason to be ashamed of your own thoughts. If you are concerned about other people reading your journal, then keep it on your person at all times.

This is a good practice anyway, as you never can tell when there might be something you want to write about.

Explore whatever topics you want. Don't limit yourself to merely journaling about your life and your feelings. Try branching out, too. Write essays on various topics of interests. For example, you could write about world hunger, the Civil War and its effect on humanity, or whatever tickles your fancy. The point here is not for you to write to receive marks or an accolade. No; the point is to spark creativity within yourself and to develop your innate potential. While writing, many things could come to you, perhaps even paradigm-altering ideas that change the way we view things. You never know! Just be true to yourself, drop whatever mask or façade you show the world, and be as authentic as you can. The only person that would be judging you is yourself, and who better to do the job? You can be your biggest cheerleader and your biggest critic, so there's nothing to be afraid of. After all, it's just you and your thoughts.

Your journal doesn't necessarily have to be in the form of written words. You could keep photography journals, voice journals, digital journals, or whatever you are comfortable with. As long as it affords you the opportunity for self-development, go for it.

NOW, REPEAT

$\mathcal{M}$ake the above processes a part of your weekly or daily routine. The clarity that comes with repeating this process is liberating as you become better at understanding yourself.

Introspection has almost become a lost art in this fast-paced world. But, if you can take some time and really connect with yourself, you will find that the blurry lines in your life come into sharper focus. With routine introspection, you will be able to make the best decisions for yourself, recognize the toxic patterns in your life, and be the best version of yourself. Beautiful things can unfold when we find out who we truly are and what we most desire!

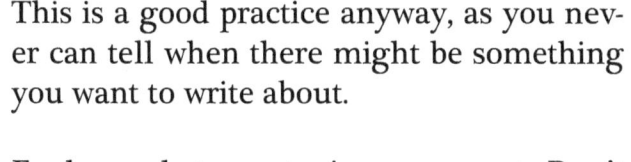

PETER McKINNON: CREATIVITY & REAL TALK!

$\mathcal{P}$eter McKinnon is a photographer, cinematographer, and all-around amazing human who I had the pleasure of working with for six years at Ellusionist. Peter ran all things visual for the company, and played a huge part in establishing the brand image. The creativity he brings to his art and life has attracted over one million subscribers to his YouTube channel, and all in less than six months.

"Creativity: are we born with it? Is it a gift? Is it something we can be taught, learn to harness, and control? Or is it something entirely different? Perhaps creativity is a scam. Maybe it's just a line used in advertising or marketing of products, something to help sell someone or an object. "From the creative mind of..." "A creative collaboration between..."

"I love you" comes to mind. Those are words that are widely and, in my opinion, loosely used. "Creativity," I feel, is a word that is also used too loosely. I think being creative and being clever are two entirely different things. Sometimes, things can be misinterpreted or targeted as being creative, when in fact they are merely clever.

"It's clever how you managed to hide that playing card." "It's clever how you thought about using a double backer instead of a double facer." Creativity is a process. Creativity is the

vehicle you ride to get to your destination. I feel like in this day and age, the term is thrown about to help boost one's image. Where that may very well apply in some cases, it most certainly does not apply to all.

I am originally a photographer. I used to shoot a lot of portraits, weddings, stock, corporate, fashion—you name it. I learned a lot about what is clever and what is creative when taking and post-processing my photos. I think when I look back at some of my photos, the entire process of how the scene was lit, shot, dreamed, etc., was creative. Where in some instances I look back and think, That was a clever use of that light stand. Ironically enough, I just did an interview segment for a local TV station on my photography endeavors, and I was asked this very same question: "How do you take creative portraits?" My answer applies to that of the magical realm as well, which we will touch on shortly.

I am blessed with being friends with many of the industry's leading minds, performers, and thinkers today. I've spent countless nights fighting exhaustion sitting with Michael Weber in a bar in Blackpool, England; jamming out fresh concepts in Las Vegas with Calen Morrelli on how to make the most insane gaff deck of cards; and spending time with underground artists such as a gentleman by the name of Shade, witnessing concepts and ideas come to life from absolutely nothing. These things happen

9

to us when we are not forcing them. That is my honest opinion. I think there are physical things humans can practice and, with repetition, they enhance and improve. I think creativity is a gift that, with time, comes to you in many different forms, some more than others.

"Think outside the box." I hate this line, and I love it at the same time. Thinking outside the box is great; we need to do it. Breaking patterns, wandering astray from the daily normalities, breaking the rules—these things help us take chances. When we do this and explore, we are made witness to new possibilities and paths we would have never been able to see or experience otherwise. However, creativity comes in when you

take that statement and turn it in on itself. Think inside the box, because everyone is too busy trying to think outside of it. I like to see what way people are going and go the opposite. I do this with almost everything. I think it's when you decide to be different and original and take chances that creativity comes over you naturally. It is all about realizing that moment of potential when it is upon you, and what you do with it when it's there.

So, do I think creativity can be practiced? Yes and no. Do I think people are naturally creative? Yes, they can be. Can creativity be taught? I think you can guide someone in the direction of thinking differently.

CONFIDENCE

Confidence is a major component of creativity that is often left by the wayside. In actuality, without this key factor, many creative ideas would die in infancy. The act of creating something, thinking about an idea, and bringing it into creation requires a level of self-acceptance and confidence that we each must discover for ourselves.

Whenever you come up with an idea, self-doubt tends to set in almost immediately, depending on how strong your inner critic is. You begin to second-guess yourself and imagine that what you have come up with is somehow inferior or not up to par with others' expectations. It takes a level of self-confidence to work past this and allow your idea to see the light of day.

Innovation is scary, like walking blindfolded into murky waters, with absolutely no sense of direction. So many of us lack the confidence to see things through, which is exactly how the world has lost track of so many creative minds.

They say self-doubt is the curse of the imaginary creative, and the fastest way to lose your self-confidence is through self-comparison. A lot of people allow themselves to play victim to self-comparison; for many of us, this is what we grow up observing in those around us. Comparing yourself to others is a bad habit that absolutely must be broken for creativity to flow.

You can compare two contradictory ideas. In fact, I encourage it! But you can't compare yourself to another individual. We are each far too complex to be compared to one another. There is no single standard for comparison. Stay guided by your own principles, inspirations, and values, rather than basing your choices on others' perceptions. Develop your skills and perfect them as much as you can. Ignore what the others are saying and give yourself peace of mind.

HOW TO MAINTAIN YOUR CONFIDENCE LEVEL: FOCUS ON YOUR ACHIEVEMENT

This is very crucial in boosting your confidence level. At some point in your life, you must have achieved something, no matter how insignificant it seemed. Revel for a moment in the successes you have found, rolling around in the joy they brought to you, even if for a moment.

Do you feel that? Do you crave it again as much as I do? Good. Find more successes. Just like in Peter Pan, think happy thoughts, and you will soar. And, like Peter Pan, focusing on the positivity and happiness you've collected with your successes will encourage you to seek similar opportunities.

PLAY TO YOUR STRENGTHS

*U*se what you have to get what you want. There's no way you're ever going to find what you're looking for in a sea of endless options. Start working with what you do have, and, just as if you were whittling down a block of wood into a sculpture, you'll soon start to find that what you've been looking for was always there.

You can't give what you don't have. To maintain your self-confidence, you have to pay more attention to your strengths. Don't allow your flaws to take center stage in your life. Focus on your strengths and work them as you would any muscle to strengthen them even more.

Work on your area of expertise, polish what you create, and make the best out of it. Don't use this as an opportunity to settle for less, however. Do your best, no matter what it is

you create, as this strengthens your self-confidence and integrity and encourages you to explore new terrain and envelop new concepts.

STAY POSITIVE

*T*he effect of positivity on one's confidence cannot be overemphasized. Maintain your level of positivity. Acknowledge that you can't always be right, you can't always get the results that you seek, and you can't always be in control of the elements in your life. Just acknowledging these things will free your mind, allowing you to find joy wherever it exists in your current life.

Worrying whether you're living or working up to someone else's standard will no longer be an issue once you relinquish your stronghold on such constraints. Likewise, any fears of rejection, judgment, or mockery will all fall by the wayside as your positivity beams through troubles like a ray of brilliant light. Once you welcome this warm source of positivity, you'll know in your heart that you will always rise up stronger and tougher for every challenge that comes your way.

CREATE WHAT SPEAKS TO YOU

*T*rends are always moving in one direction or another, but you can't base your passions or desires on these trends. You can be inspired by what others are doing, as I've mentioned before, but don't fall prey to societal conventions. If something doesn't appeal to you, don't waste your time on it. You have so much to offer the world; don't give up until you find whatever it is that speaks to you.

Find the confidence to create what you truly desire and revel in it. Enjoy the fact that you're doing what you want, rather than what others may want you to do. One of my favorite quotes by the poet Charles Bukowski says it best: "Find what you love and let it kill you." Let it destroy everything you think you know and allow it to bring ruin to whatever doesn't serve you creatively. Don't quit until you truly have found it. And you will find it.

POSITIVITY

There comes a time in each of our lives where it feels as though nothing is going right. We try our hand at so many things and hit a dead end each time. Of course, it's human nature to just want to get under the covers, curl up, and then die a slow death, but this moment is your true trial, your test of strength in the face of hardship. How will you prevail? Will you give up? Many of us, myself included, may struggle with anxiety or depression during these times, and perhaps turn to alcohol, drugs, or anything that might offer a temporary escape from reality.

What we always seem to forget during these times of struggle is that after every storm comes relief. And no matter how long the storm lasts, it will eventually stop. It's nature's way. And while we feel consumed by the emotions that plague us, our only source of hope is positivity.

We find it easy to be positive and optimistic during the good times: when we are successful, when the ideas are coming in, and when we're clearly able to consider our choices. But the moment we have a challenge on our hands, positivity seems to fly out the window, even though that's really when we need it the most.

Maintaining a positive mindset means knowing, deep down in your heart, that you have no control over the elements in your life and that sometimes these elements will even work against you, almost purposefully not giving

do you stay positive?

How do you start your morning? The way in which you kick-start your day sets the mood for how the rest of it unfolds. Do you wake up already feeling depressed or angry? Or do you wake up full of energy to face the day? Try setting the right mood for your day by injecting a healthy dose of positivity in some of these ways:

ENJOY THE LITTLE THINGS

A part of us dies when we stop seeing the extraordinary in the ordinary. We tend to focus more on the bigger achievements and pleasures of life, like buying a new house, welcoming a child, or getting married, but the sunset, walking barefoot on the beach, or watching birds in flight, can fill a person with great joy.

FIND JOY IN EVERYTHING

*T*om Wilson, the American cartoonist who created Ziggy, once said how "a smile is the happiness you find right under your nose." Smiling releases endorphins and serotonin, often referred to as our feel-good hormones. By smiling, you are actively encouraging the ideal environment for positive thoughts. Try to find joy within every moment, every thought, every facet of this wonderful life that you get to lead.

WAKE UP A WINNER

A healthy morning routine is one thing you really need to have a productive day. Start each day with a "winning" attitude. Wake up and make things happen. Surround yourself with the right vibe, utilizing morning activities that nourish your confidence and boost your energy.

STAY FOCUSED

Don't allow external forces to dictate how you feel at varying points of the day. Know that you, and you alone, can determine how you feel (and react to what you feel) throughout the day, regardless of what you are going through. Don't just lie on the ground and allow yourself to be walked over by unpleasant situations. Take back control, and decide for yourself how you want your day to flow.

INHIBIT COMPLAINING

Complaining about everything that's wrong in your life is not going to make your problems go away; if anything, it's bound to make them worse. So, instead of whining, do something about it. Shift your perspective on the matter, detach yourself from the problem, and try to find a productive solution.

INSPIRE YOURSELF

Every single day, practice positive self-talk. Much like the testimonials I write in my morning ritual, find inspiration in what already exists. If this means you have to stand in front of the mirror and tell yourself positive affirmations, do it. And while you're at it, read books with positive messages, listen to edifying music, and watch good movies.

BE REALISTIC

Most of our "problems" are just figments of our imagination. This is not to say they don't exist, but we tend to blow them just a bit out of proportion. Whether we seek attention or are trying to convince ourselves we are going through something major when we extrapolate a problem, it doesn't serve us. Rooting the mind in reality and refusing to indulge in the drama can help us find our way through struggles faster.

WATCH YOUR THOUGHTS

You are your thoughts, and whatever thoughts you allow to form in your mind will take shape in reality and affect your attitude. Choose to focus on the positive at all times. If you have the habit of thinking the worst about situations, try to inhibit the negative thoughts and promote the positive. Meditation and mindfulness are key tools to use for this practice.

GRATITUDE MEDITATION

*G*ratitude is a gracious acknowledgement of all that sustains us, a celebration of our blessings, and an appreciation of the moments of good fortune in our lives.

We have so much to be grateful for—the air we breathe, the roofs over our heads, and every other little thing we have been blessed with, so much of which we may not have necessarily earned.

You can relish the good things life has to offer and enjoy the luxury you have been afforded once you find yourself with gratitude. With gratitude comes joy, and a joyous heart is a positive heart.

You'll be able to enjoy moments spent with loved ones, friends, pets, and so on, because you'll understand what a privilege each experience truly is. It's a gift to be alive, and once you embrace this fact, you'll find yourself more contented with what you have, rather than chasing after clouds. In essence, you'll lead a rich life.

Ask yourself what you're grateful for. Write these as testimonials, if it helps you. Just ensure you take time out of your busy schedule to think about the things you're grateful for in your life. You will find yourself acknowledging that nothing lasts forever, thereby allowing yourself to fully embrace and enjoy what you do have.

DAN HARLAN: SPEAKS ON CREATIVITY

*D*an Harlan is a magician, inventor, and entertainer. Dan has invented more magic than just about anyone alive. He's well known internationally for his insanely creative contributions to the magic community. If you want to know something about magic, you can pretty much guarantee that Dan will have the answer. His knowledge of the art is rivaled by none, and he has a very unique and refreshing take on what it means to be creative.

ADAM: How did you choose your creative outlet?

DAN: Do you mean "magic," or "art," or "writing," or "cooking," or "acting," or... I didn't consciously choose any of my creative endeavors. I simply love to do many creative things.

A: What inspires you?

D: Inspiration can come from anywhere and anything at any time. Really, I can't force it, predict it, or define it. Early on, a lot of my inspiration came from recreational mathematics because that's what I was reading at the time. Then, I got into design, symbology, physics, and psychology. There are so many fascinating aspects of our world that can inspire us when we allow them to.

A: How do you define creativity?

D: Creativity is our innate ability to play.

A: Do you believe each person has the capacity to be creative? Why?

D: Yes, as I mentioned in my definition, it is an innate ability. As children, we engage in creative thought as we encounter everything for the first time. Eventually, the rules of society constrain our thinking by replacing our need for creativity with an ordered system. However, our desire for play remains intact, and it's the role of creative artists to provide us with new and interesting options for expressing this desire.

A: How did you find your creative niche?

D: I followed my own desire for interesting expressions.

A: Who or what experiences have inspired your work?

D: Everyone and everything. Sounds glib, perhaps, but it is the truth.

A: Have you always wanted to do what you are doing? If not, what made you decide to start?

D: I have been quite fortunate that I have been able to do what I love. There have been very few times when I was required to temporarily squelch my spirit and conform, but given the choice, I always chose the path less traveled.

A: Do spirituality and culture play a role in your creativity? Explain.

D: Yes. As I mentioned, everything influences my process. In my work, you will find references to life, death, love, happiness, sadness, loneliness, family, etc. Typically, I prefer these universal themes to remain subtle, but occasionally I'll write a piece that overtly deals with an issue.

A: How important is education to your creative process?

D: Unfortunately, standard educational models encourage a rote memorization and regurgitation of facts. My education involved hours of research outside school investigating concepts, theories, and experiments which would give the facts some much needed context, as well as open pathways of exploration that would reveal unexpected connections. In other words: play. I highly recommend supplemental, individual studies to anyone wishing to have a thorough education.

A: How do you deal with creativity blocks?

D: I dig in my "Brain Box"—it's an index card file in which I've written down and categorized every fleeting idea I feel might have a future, so that later (like when I'm stuck), I can take the time to develop the ideas. It's the most basic tool any creative person should employ: write it down. I also have plastic bags filled with prototypes that I work on from time to time.

A: What part of you do you share in your creative endeavors?

D: Whichever part fits the task at hand.

A: Have you had to overcome obstacles (physical, financial, social, etc.) in your creative world? Explain.

D: I am of average intelligence, from an average family with average financial means and social status. Yes, I've overcome obstacles by making the most of whatever I have. I don't think I've ever triumphed over adversity, nor have I been given a free ride. What I have, I've earned. I consider myself fortunate.

A: Do you believe it's important to be accepted by others as being creative, or is just doing what you love to do enough to justify your work? Explain.

D: For me, the acceptance of others is such an important gauge of the quality of my work that I can't imagine being without it. Perhaps if I lived isolated on a tiny island, relying on my ingenuity for my survival, I wouldn't care what anyone else thought, as long as I lived. However, since I offer my creations as viable solutions for a group of discerning individuals, I believe it is my responsibility to listen to their feedback. Now, that doesn't mean I will base what I do on isolated commentary. Not even close. I still have my own opinion (based on a wealth of knowledge and experience) to guide me, but it is important to me that my success can be measured by the satisfaction of others.

THE FOLLOWING IS AN EXCERPT FROM MORE THAN MEETS THE EYE BY: DAN HARLAN

"Creativity resists structure. It needs openness and room to move freely from concept to concept. It is chaotic and unpredictable. If you arrive at a foregone conclusion, ending up where you decided to go, then you are not being creative. Creativity is a journey with no map, no destination, no agenda, no schedule, and no expectations. Just hop in your car and go. Better yet, walk, or ride a horse, or a motorcycle, or a bicycle, or fly a plane, or hot air balloon.

The balloon is probably best since you have the least control and you just have to take the scenery as it comes. Your mind is now open and directionless, filled with unrelated ideas with no structure. This is great! This is inspirational! This is a big waste of time!

There is a problem with pure creativity. Nothing ever gets done. You can create in your unlimited imagination forever, but what then? If you try to present an audience with your wandering mental processes, what will they think? It will make no sense. You must take the results from your journey (snapshots, if you will) and put them in a structured order into your scrapbook, so it all makes sense. Throw out the boring ones, or the blurry ones, or the poorly developed ones. Keep only those images that support your central theme. The reason most vacation pictures are boring is because there is no interesting theme, except, "Look how much fun we had while you were here working your butt off."

Entertainment comes in various forms to suit a variety of tastes and interests. Treat your performance as a piece of music, or a painting, or a sporting event, or a book, or a meal. Some

people prefer pork, or poetry, or pole vaulting, or Picasso, or punk rock. Some don't. No matter what though, everything has its own style and an audience which values it. Do you have your own style? Everyone does, but is it the one you want your audience to see? The best way to develop your style is through your script. The words, actions, emotions, and expressions you use comprise your script, whether you have written it down or not.

This is a performance, after all. It is theater. You are acting. You have an audience. Even if you are doing a pocket trick for a friend, you have the same opportunities and responsibilities as the performer in a Grand Stage Musical Spectacular Extravaganza televised to millions. You both can succeed or fail based on your interpretation of your script. I suggest that you study what you can about the theater and how plays

movies, or television shows are put together. I prefer to study live theater since that is mainly what we do, and it is the basis of all other performances.

It has a long and fascinating history. You may choose to read about its history, or study a few scripts from the library to see how they are written, or better yet, you may join an amateur theatrical group for some firsthand experience. There are many capacities in which to work, both onstage and off, but you will learn more than you ever thought possible no matter whether you're in front of the lights or behind them. "

21

CURIOSITY

$\mathcal{F}$ar too many of us are afraid of our curious tendencies and don't follow them as a result. To open yourself to creativity, you have to follow your curiosity streak, and almost fanatically so. The importance of asking the right questions can't be emphasized enough. The act of innovation—of creating something truly innovative—can only be achieved when you continuously seek to know more.

Who are the most curious creatures? Children. Their instinctive curiosity is why they are so much more readily able to identify problems that adults will generally dismiss. Children can hold a conversation revolving around five different subjects in the space of a few minutes. They jump seamlessly from one topic to the other, often leaving the adults around them reeling from the shock of it all. And though this can be quite frustrating for any parent, it's wildly fascinating if you encourage it.

When you train your mind to be receptive like that of a child, you'll be open to new ideas, never dismissing them outright as stupid. In this way, then, you'll be free to be curious about different things and, thus, continuous-

ly opening yourself up to new experiences. Curiosity is the key that opens the doors to enlightenment. This will, in turn, lead to the development of creative solutions.

Challenge yourself. Maybe you'll find that you can't do certain things, or maybe you'll find that you can. Either way, you'll never know until you try. Your mind knows no bounds except for those you construct; let yourself ponder anything and everything that rises to the surface.

If answers come to you without much effort, then they've probably dawned on others in a similar way. When this happens, dig deeper: ask more questions and explore critical answers to stand out from the herd. What you find doesn't always have to make sense. The

connections that sometimes exist between seemingly unrelated things are crucial when applied to thinking creatively and opening the doors to innovation. Curiosity can lead to game changing ideas if given a chance to flourish.

Children reap the benefits that come as the result of having a healthy appetite for curiosity, and so should we as adults. We need to work on finding and sustaining ways of rewarding ourselves for being curious and allowing our minds the space and right to conceive.

In addition to asking a lot of questions, ask a lot of open-ended questions. Kids are the best at this, and often do so to the point of exhaustion. Ensure your questions are not restricted or controlled. Ask open-ended questions, and then allow your mind to acknowledge and accept any of the solutions that arise.

It's all too easy to become mired in the existing definition of "normal." Think about the great people, past and present, who have im-

pacted the world in some profound way. How did they do it? The answer is simple: they were curious and refused to believe what existed was the very best we could have. They questioned the status quo and were able to discover better ways of doing things not just for their own benefit, but for everyone's.

Life is dull and monotonous for some, but not for the curious. How can it be? Well, they don't allow themselves to get so desensitized that their sense of wonder disappears. For them, there are always new things that deserve their attention. They lead adventurous lives because as far as they are concerned, life itself is an adventure.

Ultimately, those with curiosity are the ones who change the world, because they are always asking the all-important questions that begin with "why."

NAVIGATE ENVIRONMENTAL FACTORS

*Y*our thoughts and ideas are direct products of your work environment. You draw energy and motivation from your surroundings, and working in that right place is probably all that is standing between you and your creative breakthrough. Of course, what you draw motivation from depends on who you are. While some people can only work in pristine and shining environments, others find they think better amidst light chaos.

According to a paper published in the Journal of Environmental Psychology, darkness and dim lighting can encourage freedom of thoughts, which leads to a more prolific generation of ideas. This conclusion was reached because dim lighting would reduce the visibility of the distractions available in a room, thus encouraging focus on internal reflection and the task at hand. This isn't to say that bright ideas will only come to you in a dimly lit room. What will ultimately work best for you will be determined by you alone, and probably after a couple of trial-and-error tests.

Let's examine F. Scott Fitzgerald, the author of Tender is the Night, an autobiographical novel about the physical, financial, and moral decline of a man with nearly limitless potential. It was reported that while he was working on this novel, he and his wife, Zelda, moved between France, Switzerland, and the United States, and eventually spent eighteen months at La Paix, an old country house north of Baltimore, Maryland. He was said to have worked through the night in a dark, disheveled room with a bottle of gin in a nearby drawer. He would take short walks and come back to jot down his ideas on notepads scattered across his desk. Clearly, Fitzgerald found motivation in mild chaos and after long walks. He came upon most of his more successful ideas by working in an environment that suited him and his needs.

On the other hand, some people have reported that merely looking at a messy desk puts them off and throws them off their game. So, working in a cluttered workspace wouldn't be to their advantage. Find out (if you don't already have a good idea) what type of workspace will inspire the most
creativity and run with it. Some people work better in clean spaces with minimal art on the walls while others thrive at messy desks in cluttered offices.

Aside from the ambience, consider how convenient the workspace is. Would you be able to reach for important things easily, or would it be a battle to be productive? If you needed to carry out natural bodily functions, would you have to go too far outside of your workspace to do so? Do you have refreshments available, or do you need to leave your space to go find some grub? Your output depends on how convenient your working environment is. Imagine working in a place where there was no proper air conditioning system, not even a fan, and the heat level was high. (I sincerely hope that none of you do.) Of course, you would be sweaty and uncomfortable. Under such conditions, chances are you'd never be productive. So, for your own good, equip your space with the things you know you will need, and do so in a way that promotes productivity and efficiency. The lit-

tle things add up, and they go a long way.

If you discover that you are not getting the feel you want from your current workspace, get out of it. Try out new spaces, especially ones that inspire creativity. Some people have been reported getting some of their best ideas while watching people move about in the park, or while watching people interact in coffee shops. So, get out and break the pattern your brain is used to, so you can see things from a different vantage point.

If you can afford it, travel to places you've always wanted to go, or return to a place you remember with fondness. If the culture there is different from what you're used to, even better. It's all about gaining new insights and perspectives on things. Watching the way things are done by other people brings about a new level of awareness, which is, of course, the ultimate goal.

BRAD CHRISTIAN: COUNTERACT THE FEAR OF FAILURE

*B*rad is the founder of the world's largest and oldest online magic store, Ellusionist. Brad has been my boss, friend, and mentor for many years. I have learned so much from picking his brain about everything from investments to packaging design for products. Brad sees this world differently than anyone else I've ever met.

"To me, creativity seems to be an expression of letting your imagination flow. Get rid of the boxes around things; get rid of your thoughts about the way things "have to be" or "should be." Try several different avenues for the same thing; experiment. Use a lot of "what-if" scenarios. Trick your mind into letting go of its natural boundaries. If you can, try to make a mock-up of the thing you are thinking of, so you can see it, feel it, and play with it. Even doing that may lead you to take a different approach.

Mostly, don't be afraid to fail. Counteract the fear of failure by telling yourself how many times the greats failed before they came up with the very thing that made them great. Failing is a part of the success process. You have to put a certain number of failures into the mix to ensure success. They're like stairs. Every time you fail, it creates another stair

you step on to get you closer to your goal.

Lastly, remember that the creation process often requires you to simply let go. You try and try and try and get all wound up in a ball. Your head is tight and knotted up. LET. GO. Do something different. It could be that the tightness of trying so hard is keeping the idea from coming through. Some of the best ideas come when you are on a walk by yourself. Movement allows flow. Don't be bothered if you look hard for an idea and it just isn't there. It can come in a second. That empty space can fill up in a moment. Just wait. The idea is already sitting there; YOU just have to arrive."

COMBAT PROCRASTINATION

How many times have you said, "I'll do it!" and then you never get to it? How many times were you supposed to apply for something, but pushed it until the very last minute when there was absolutely nothing that could be done about it?

I cringe when I think about the number of opportunities that have been lost, not because the individual in question didn't have what it took to get it done, but because he or she procrastinated so much that there was no choice between success and failure.

Time is something we can't explain, and yet somehow, we often think we can mold it into whatever we want it to be. A lot of people find succor in postponing things until tomorrow, when they can easily be done today. When you get comfortable with procrastination, such that it becomes second nature, you have then closed the tap that accommodates your creativity and rendered it homeless.

When it is indeed time to get things done, sometimes you hit a roadblock or just lose interest in the entire thing. Instead of throwing in the towel and waiting until another day, have inspirational items at hand to keep you

occupied through the block. Whether this is a painting, sculpture, toy, book, or just a quote on your wall, know what works for you and maximize the opportunity.

One of the greatest disservices you can do to yourself is to doubt the efficacy of your journey and whether you have what it takes to make it over the finish line. You've come so far, and you've done it through sheer grit and determination, because you do have what it takes to be a success. Tune out the negativity that pervades our world, and be positive that you were made with an overwhelming capacity to be creative and innovative.

Some routines are essential in giving our lives order. To prevent procrastination, create an easy-to-follow routine to start each day or creative session. Perhaps this is the routine I delve into in the other section of this book.

Whatever you choose, once you start, stick with it and don't allow yourself to lose days here and there. Start by setting a target for your early morning. It could be something as simple as jogging for a mile, meditating for fifteen minutes, or listening to (or reading) an inspirational text.

When you stick with the routine, day in day out, and meet with your target even though no one is watching, you'll start each day successfully. When this happens, you'll begin to believe more boldly in the ability you have to stick with something and get it done. You'll train your mind to know that you can succeed and finish other tasks.

There's no hard and fast rule for these things, and nor is there a set-in-stone method of getting things done. Realize that you don't have to start at the beginning simply because everyone else does. Just like creating a magic trick, sometimes you start at the end and work your way backwards. Maybe that's the method that works for you; don't get lost in another's methods—even mine!

Your creative mode will not get turned on ev-

ery time, so when it does, immerse yourself in it and don't allow for any outside distractions at that time. Disconnect from all things that have the power to divert your focus: turn off your phone, close your computer tabs, and forget about the existence of Facebook and Twitter for that stretch of time. Your chats will not go anywhere; concentrate on what you have to do and block the rest out.

In addition, don't fall into the trap of trying to multitask. When in the zone of concentration, some people try to do as many things as possible at once, ostensibly to save time. This only muddies the water, however. Focus on what you have to do and get it done, efficiently and effectively.

TAKE RISKS

There's absolutely nothing wrong with being an employee of an organization that pays for your services, so long as when you wake up each day, it's with a spring in your step. No matter what it is that tickles your fancy, follow it through! Embody it! Then, once you find it, push yourself to be your best.

If you want to go out on a limb and awaken your creativity, you don't have to give up every stable thing in your life to do so. Some people quit their jobs and redefine their lives in a big way because they want to heed their creative voices, and a lot of change needs to be made to do so. But this definitely doesn't have to be the case for you.

When you allow your creativity to take hold, you put yourself out into the world and you open yourself up to criticism and commentary, which can be terrifying. You run the risk of being judged and critiqued, and your motives analyzed by others.

When you come at creativity from a place of fear, you'll be incapable of giving your best and could possibly compromise your vision. Instead, be confident in the person you are. Know that you have the raw materials required for success, and leave yourself open to hearing the voice of the universe.

Confidence is a state of believing in yourself, and if you're going to face yourself and the world, it's a weapon you need to have in your arsenal. Trust yourself, trust your guts, and feel free to accept praise when you deserve it. Take a deep breath and take the necessary step outside of your comfort zone. I guarantee you: there are no guarantees. It may work, and it may not. Understand that whatever sides the dice land on, you're a success for trying, and you'll be better off in

the end for the experience.

Get comfortable with failure. Of course, that isn't to say seek it out; rather, get to a place in your life where you're not afraid of failure. And remember that in so many of these failures are hidden gems of success. Forage, find those successes, and build upon them.

A lot of people will spend a lifetime going through the motions, doing what everyone else expects rather than what they actually want to do. They err on the side of caution all their lives because they're constantly buried under the weight of other's opinions of them. These people forget how to speak the language of their soul because they're worried about everyone else. People will talk, no matter what you do, and it will usually run the gamut from good, to bad, and back again. Their opinions are as fickle as the weather. Why, then, would you want to follow a blueprint of your life as designed by these people? Don't be deterred from your true path by other's judgments.

Every creative endeavor requires that you make a choice between taking the risky route and remaining in the same place. It can be hard to face our fears, insecurities, and seeming inadequacies, but that is what creativity demands. We must stand before a mirror, look critically at ourselves and our surroundings, and get tough about it. Creativity demands that you face your fears and act confidently in the face of reality. So, no more cowering in the face of conflict. No more withering under pressure. No. Stand up, put your foot down, and guide your creative fire through this crazy world.

Taking big risks and putting yourself on the line demands that you face your personal demons. Just remember: when you're looking in the face of your shadow self, that which you fear also empowers you. Be your shadow self's own worst enemy, and rip those fears and inadequacies to shreds. Take ownership of your livelihood, and walk forward boldly.

TAKE CARE OF YOURSELF

Your self-care routine will be your road to creativity, so long as you keep it well paved. Don't let yourself relinquish the need for basic human necessities just because you're creative. Those stereotypical creatives didn't need to struggle so hard to unearth their creative genius and probably could've done a bit better with an extra shower here or there, anyway.

Take note of the following, and ensure you don't forego supplying yourself with whatever it is you need to maintain a status quo of creative capability.

GET ENOUGH SLEEP

Lack of sufficient sleep leads to negative effects on creativity. Depriving yourself of even a single night's rest could impair your abilities to make decisions and think creatively. Sleeping gives your brain the rest it needs. After all, the brain is the biggest creative tool, so it's quite advantageous to rest it.

Some people pull all-nighters during brainstorming sessions, depriving their body of the sleep it craves. Usually, nothing too productive comes of such brainstorming sessions, as the brain is most likely out of juice after a short while. Don't forget that you can't cheat nature. If you deprive your body of something as natural as sleep, you'll have to pay for it later, and by then, it could be too out of your control to do anything about.

As well as getting enough sleep, try using the tools below to ensure you get the proper kind of sleep each night:

STICK TO A SCHEDULE

Set a time limit for you to work. When it ends, stop whatever it is you're doing and start preparing for bed. This would mean you need to complete all the work that has been allocated for that day before it's time for bed. Avoid procrastination as much as possible, so you don't have to rush through your work, or carry it over to the next day. While deciding on a time to stop working, make sure you allow yourself at least seven hours for sleep. Whatever you decide, just make sure to pick a schedule that works for you and stick to it.

PREPARE YOURSELF

Right before you actually go to bed, do something to get in the mood. Try something relaxing, so that when you eventually pull the covers over your body and let your head hit the pillow, you will have a restful sleep. Some people have reported that when they sleep, they dream about their work and at the end of the night wake up rather frustrated and tired. To avoid this, do something to take the stress of the day away. Take a long shower, and if you are into meditation, do so for a few minutes before bed. Read a book, take a bath, smoke some herb, put some lavender on your pillow and breathe it in, or anything else that will lull you into sleepy-time.

AVOID STIMULANTS

As much as you can, avoid stimulants before going to bed. They can deprive you of the sleep you need. If and when you eventually do fall asleep, you may end up not getting the relaxing and refreshing effect that comes from a good night's rest. Excessive drinking before bed will only give you a terrible hangover the next morning, and this will obviously limit your productivity that day.

STAY AWAY FROM SCREENS

For about two hours before you sleep, log off the Internet on your computer and avoid browsing social media feeds or replying your emails at that time. Turn off the television, too, and let your brain breathe easy. If you go straight to bed after going through your Facebook feed, there's the possibility that your mind will be pondering something you saw there as you dream, without any conscious effort on your part. And we really want to keep our sleep, and our dreams, as clean as we can at all times.

STAY ACTIVE AND HEALTHY

Your health is your wealth, and a healthy you is one of the greatest contributions you can make to your community. When not weighed down by illness, you can be proactive, affording yourself the opportunity to make meaningful contributions to mankind. Making any meaningful contributions from a hospital bed might be a little impossible, if not entirely so.

Eat a healthy, balanced diet. Avoid things that would damage your health like cigarettes and drugs, and maintain a healthy body weight. Try working out as much as you can, go on long, cleansing walks, take the stairs more often, and generally do things that will ensure you are in good shape.

INNOVATE

*C*reativity and innovation are linked, and there is no way one can exist without the other. Innovation is the birth of creativity—creativity coming to fruition. Innovation means turning the impossible around and redefining it. Innovation is spinning ideas into reality, like Rumpelstiltskin did straw into gold. All innovation begins with creative thinking, coupled with creative ideas, and followed by massive action.

Successful people are comfortable with failure. They know, in trying to be true to themselves and do great things, they will make some mistakes. Fail with your idea over and over again until it becomes something truly innovative—until it becomes a success.

Steve Jobs said in 1997 that "creativity is just connecting things." Creative people are able to draw lines between different things, connecting totally unrelated ideas to create new ones. While some people are innately in touch with their creativity, others of us tend to lose sight of it from time to time… and often when we need it the most!

Ideas are great, amazing things, but don't allow yourself to get so hung up on an initial idea that you can't improve. This is where true innovation is found, after all: in the fight, the struggle, the uncomfortable wrestling with what it is and what could be. For this reason, the single most important companion to have on the way to innovation is creativity.

You don't have to be an expert; you can create something new in any field, just so long as you have the inspiration needed to develop new ideas and the bravery to struggle with what you create.

MARC SPELMANN: NOT ALL BRAINS WORK THE SAME

*M*arc Spelmann is a mentalist out of the UK. His contributions to the world of magic and mentalism are colossal. People in the industry of the impossible know of his work, and for good reason. Marc is a performer whom I have looked up to for many years. I just love the way his brain observes problems, then beats them to death until they reincarnate as solutions.

" I have always been classified as a creator and performer by my peers within the magic industry. I started out performing as an enthusiastic kid, always fascinated with special effects and magic principles. I was always dreaming up ways of creating ghostly apparitions, moving objects and oddities that would baffle the adults around me. I was an unconventional child and am now an unconventional adult.

I had a built-in brain for magic as a child, but I wasn't well read, in that I didn't own any magic books or have anyone in my family with an association to show biz, let alone magic. Yet I was always baffled at the reactions of my family when a magician was on television. For whatever reason, I simply knew how things worked, what the magician was doing, and, in most cases, I could replicate the close-up pieces. I vividly remember watching David Copperfield's Vanishing Statue of Liberty and knowing the exact method—the same with his Death Saw illusion, Timothy Wenk's Misled (pencil through bank note), and

countless other illusions and close-up demonstrations, I say that with the utmost respect for those outstanding, beautiful pieces of magic which have inspired me greatly. I don't really know why or how, but I just knew what was happening. I think in some ways you need to think outside of the box and have a topological brain.

The reason I am writing this is to emphasize a simple fact: not all brains work the same. If they did, we would all play the piano and be scholars. The fact is, we all see things differently, are inspired by different things, and, to be more specific in relation to our topic, our creativity will be born from different things. I can only relay what works for me and the process I go through to create. For ease of reading and reference, I will categorize them below. You may find some of these work for you or you do them already. They aren't rocket science, but just the various ways I get creative.

Your environment: Creativity can come at any time. You could be sitting on the beach, stuck in traffic, or in the gym lifting weights when an idea just pops in your head. For me, this is how most of my creative ideas happen. Something just clicks, and an idea is born, sometimes leading to a full-fledged effect I use, or other times ending up as an idea written in my notebooks.

But what about when we have to be creative? What if we have a show that needs that great ending; a quick, dynamic opener; a script for that PK effect; or something new for our close-up set? Everyone will be different, as stated before, but my personal preference is a good coffee shop, a comfy sofa, and my iPad or a notebook with some inspirational, lifting music. I'm essentially taking myself away from regular distractions in my life. I'm away from my office with just some music to take me somewhere and my mind. Whatever you need to do to feel comfortable and prepared, do it. You wouldn't go to the gym in boots and a fur coat—you would prepare yourself, and the same should apply to creating. Get in the zone in whatever way you need—music, solitude, maybe daydreaming or relaxing in the tub.

It doesn't matter what, how, or where. Just give yourself some space to go inwards.

Just write something: This is something I learnt from a dear friend many years ago. Rather than stare at a blank page, it's better to write everything down, even if it's something you know will be scrapped. Just write it down. I do this with everything—scripts, routines, methods, procedures, etc. I just write and write; inevitably most of it will be changed, rewritten, or scrapped, but sometimes the hardest thing to do with anything is to actually start. Don't worry if it doesn't make sense or seems outlandish, unachievable, or silly. Just write it down, and it may inspire you and lead to something else or, at the very worst, just be erased.

When I created Transmission from Chapter One of my DVD set, The Chapters of Marc Spelmann, it came to life by my wanting a drawing duplication set that was totally impromptu—no devices, gimmicks, etc. I wanted something I could do anywhere, at any time, as long as there were paper and pens.

I listed my requirements, then went through every method in my mind. It took a while, but once I hit on the method, I was so inspired. I love that routine and so do many others, including my friend Banachek, who put it in Psychological Subtleties 3.

Write and walk away: Sometimes when we get stuck, we come to what marathon runners call "the wall." It is quite literally the most frustrating thing. My advice is walk away. Go to the gym, go to the cinema, and just get away from what you are trying to do. Frustration leads to anger, anger clouds the mind, and forcing ideas isn't enjoyable and is often a waste of time. It is far better to take a breather, have some fun, and come back after a day or two.

I have a newspaper prediction which had to be solo operational, in that I couldn't use assistants. It had to be straightforward and direct. I read everything I could, including old manuscripts, books, and notes, but it just wouldn't click. I walked away and literally forgot about it for six months, and then one day it just fell into

place. The effect was born in 2002, it then led to my Prize Draw routine.

Which comes first? I always hear this debate from colleagues and associates: "Do you think of the routines first, then decide on the method, or do you have a method that then leads to a routine?"

This is a very good question, but it has no answer as both occur in equal measure. Most of the time, I dream up the routine or effect I'd like to be able to achieve, then continue to find a suitable method or methods; sometimes, I even discover a method or technique that's amazing. With the latter scenario, I find myself searching for a place to use this method, applying it to a routine. This isn't a bad thing, as, to be honest, how we get to the finishing post is unimportant, as long as we get there if it's a routine, then method, or method turning into a routine, who cares? Sometimes a method will spark creativity, thought, and possibilities which will only assist in helping us develop more individually.

If it ain't broke, don't fix it! I think this is by far the most ridiculous statement ever made — most likely by some lazy person who had no vision. If we didn't develop, advance, and progress, we'd still be sitting in candlelight and cooking on log fires. Always analyze everything you do, and, by all means, fix things, even if the old version works. Sometimes we need to move forward and try a new approach, method, or device. Anything that gets our brains ticking is a good thing. Sure, it won't always be relevant or required with certain effects, but, to be honest, I can't think of a routine that I haven't fixed or adjusted, even when it was getting the reactions I wanted.

Those are a few paragraphs that may help with creativity and development. It may just be a section you skipped, which means you won't have read this bit either. Regardless, I wish you the very best with whatever you do, create, invent, or develop.

GET INSPIRED

*I*nspiration! The bedrock for any creative breakthrough. Some of the time, inspiration can come to us in the form of a "light-bulb moment," hitting us over the head with ideation. But more often than not, this isn't the case. In fact, inspiration will often arise due to a great deal of sheer conscious effort.

Waiting for inspiration to find you can be just that: a waiting game. Rather than wait around until inspiration waddles its way over to you, try sitting down for a brainstorming session, where you call upon inspiration or perhaps go digging for it all on your own.

Not everyone will have the proverbial "light-bulb moment," so inspiration will have to be sought after, both within and without. You will have to look within yourself to find out what makes you who you are, what you are passionate about, and what interests and fascinates you, for in all these things, you will find your source of inspiration. In other words, push your own buttons and really dig into getting to know yourself. If you can find your own unique identity in this ever-changing world, then you will be your own source of inspiration.

Introspection is the examination of one's own conscious thoughts and feelings. Ask yourself important self-revealing questions, such as:

- **Who am I?**

- **What matters most to me?**

- **What do I want to change in my environment?**

- **What is my purpose here?**

A lot of people would generally run away from asking themselves such questions, as discovering one's true self is really one of the greatest challenges we face as individuals. The life hack here is to overcome this challenge, because you will then discover a new part of yourself to explore.

Meditation can help a lot on this journey of self-discovery through introspection. Calming the mind and ridding it of the constant babble is advisable to connect with one's self on a deep level. They say the best way to get things done is to not do anything at all for a while. This is where meditation comes in: de-stimulating the brain. Through meditation, you will be able to quiet the constant chatter of the mind, bringing in focus, insight,

and calmness. What meditation does is blur the unimportant things, bringing the important ones into sharper focus, so we can best manifest what we most desire.

To get started, try spending at least twenty minutes each morning meditating. Try focusing on the sensation of your breathing, and that alone. Try not to get caught up in your thoughts. Rather, allow your every thought to float away as it comes to you. Acknowledge it, and then release it. Don't hold onto anything. If it's worthwhile, it'll come back! Empty your mind, and allow the calm to take over your body. You will feel the difference for the rest of the day.

THINK LIKE A CHILD

*B*ecooming an adult has its luxuries and freedoms, but it also possesses its fair share of responsibilities and regulations. Often, these regulations can feel a bit like strangulations, keeping us at an arm's length from what we most desire.

Children are more pure and raw in their interactions with the world. They're generally less fearful of persecution or judgement, as they're mostly unaware of its existence when it's present. Children are generally more authentic and changeable, not regulated by the

static rules our society demands we follow.

There are few adults who can say with all sincerity that they don't care about what others think of them. Most of us do; we carry the weight of others' opinions around and allow it to drown out our own authentic voices.

Children are able to live out their dreams. They don't see anything they create as unrealistic or impossible. Life seems like a marvelous, magical place when viewed through the lens of childhood. This lens is similar to the one we should adopt when we dig into our creativity.

The dynamics of this perception change as we mature. We become bogged down by the responsibilities we face, and we stop daydreaming; we stop playing and we, in turn, forget how to be creative. That childlike mentality fades away and falls into the background of our daily lives. It disappears as we become bound to our responsibilities. We become blinded by everything else around us

and just try to do our best to hang on for this wild ride.

You're an adult, and there's no going back, even though so many of us wish we could! So, how can you be or think more like a child? The first step is daydreaming. Your adult mind might think it silly and maybe even a waste of time, but daydreaming has been found to enhance creativity. When you exist in this state, it acts as a stress reliever and prevents you from getting stuck in monotonous routines. Contrary to adult opinion, daydreaming does not detract from productivity; it can actually help you become more productive.

You don't have to spend the better part of your day daydreaming to enhance creativity. Fifteen-minute daydreaming breaks are all you really need to open your mind to new ideas. This helps you visualize your dreams and goals as a reality, as well. When you allow yourself to daydream, you're able to focus more on the intangible nature of your goal and really dig into the questions that most leave unanswered.

Do yourself a favor: look at the things that interest you and actually be interested in them. Learn more than their surface features. Take things a step further and find out why and how they work. Don't stop until you get to the end of the line and there are no longer any questions on your mind.

Play with the elements of the life you're leading. Allow yourself the freedom to let go and engage your mind creatively with what's in front of you. When children play, they superimpose their thoughts on their reality such that in their minds, they become one and the same. When children play, they don't spend time thinking about the consequences of what they do or say. They don't care how they will be viewed, as they aren't trying to impress anyone. They're only trying to have fun.

While we don't want to completely relinquish our wise, educated, mature minds, we do want to open the doors to our creativity and give it a chance to really flow when we give ourselves moments to be free and act like children.

Experiment and try new things. One of the killers of creativity, and the rut we so often fall into as adults, is the comfortable feeling we get from being in the same place and doing the same things over and over again. As we live in our safe zones, we get comfortable with our routines and hesitate to try things that are unfamiliar to us. We

forget that in unfamiliarity, something truly beautiful might develop.

Try some new food, experiment with a foreign language, go places you wouldn't normally go, take classes, meet new people… immerse yourself in another's way of life. These activities can take you out of your comfort zone and cast you into regions previously unknown or unexplored, for the unknown is the birthplace of creative expression.

READ

Readers are leaders, they say, and they tell no lies. Reading, here, isn't about reading press releases, blog entries, or newspaper articles; rather, try to focus on novels, audiobooks, and other more juicy, absorbable bits of information. Fiction, motivational self-help, autobiography—whatever tickles your fancy, really. Reading books helps to improve creativity in a number of ways by:

IMPROVING CONCENTRATION

Just like meditating, reading a book will improve your power of concentration. We live in a fast-paced world, with so many activities going on and various distractions like the Internet, television, video games, etc. A good book is the perfect way to disconnect from all of these. Even if it is just for a short period of time, your brain will surely thank you for it.

EXERCISING YOUR BRAIN

You'll find reading to be a leisurely and easy way to exercise your brain. We have grown accustomed to exercising our bodies and neglecting our minds. Mental fitness is just as important as physical fitness; some would argue that it is even more so. Reading exercises our mind and improves our imagination, making us think and even fantasize about different scenarios. So many of my great ideas have struck me while reading (or in my case, listening) to a good ol' book!

RELIEVING STRESS

A tired mind can't come up with a great idea; it just doesn't work that way. Research has proven that reading is a highly effective way of relieving stress. Allowing yourself to get caught up in a book can distract you from your immediate environment, often helping

accumulated tension to dissipate. This form of escapism is practiced by many people.

Every book you read is like a database of information, just waiting for you to tap into it. Books are a window to the world outside of yourself. From the comfort of wherever you are reading, you can travel to various parts of the world, experience cultural diversity, and learn about the different people in different places and their way of life, thus broadening your scope on life.

The advantages of reading are numerous. It is advisable to read at least fifteen minutes a day to boost brain activity. Read on, friends. Read on.

ACTUALIZE YOUR MAGIC

*A*ssumption is the fastest killer of creativity, and it's so easy for us to assume. Much easier than trying to get to the real root of a problem, define it, and assess the reality of how best to solve it, that's for sure.

Assumptions lead us nowhere, save for the trappings of constant struggle. You see, when we make assumptions, our fate is already decided, and we fail to actually address what's happening. To come up with a truly creative and innovative solution to any problem, one must come to understand the actual truths of the problems one faces.

There are certain assumptions that need to be challenged if we intend to fire up our creative juices. These include, but are most definitely not limited to, thinking that:

- **A certain idea would take too much time to create and might not be worth it in the long run.**

- **We will be unable to find the resources we need to actualize our idea.**

- **Things must follow a particular pattern, and deviating from the pattern**

wouldn't yield a result.

• **An idea must be wrong if no one else has thought of it yet.**

• **We won't be able to craft the idea ourselves.**

Assumptions will prevent us from exploring our possibilities because we have already limited the playing field. So instead of having, say, a whole world of options at our disposal, we are limited to work with what's left after our assumptions have gobbled up so much of the goodness.

Why do people find it safer to assume things rather than to actually investigate?

Primarily, the fear of failure inhibits us from moving past our assumptions. You may carry the fear of being mocked or publicly ridiculed. The fear of being judged is a natural one, especially when trying out new things. But how will we ever stand out if we always assume the worst?

Our inner critic plays a major role in the assumptions we make by interference. While it's good to be your best critic when coming up with creative ideas, it's essential to tame this side of us if it should begin to get out of control.

For example, you could come up with an idea, and your inner critic could say to you: "That is a really stupid idea. How did you come up with something like that?" We all have these moments of doubt, but how much credence do we give this inner voice in the end? Our idea could turn out to be stupid, but we can only know this after the idea has been seen through to completion—not while it is still in its infancy.

So, how do we tame our inner critic and prevent it from interfering? These few tips should help:

RECORD EVERY THOUGHT

*D*uring a brainstorming session, a lot of ideas will come to you, and you may be tempted to discard some of them based on the assumption that they're bad ideas, but the secret here is not to. Silence the critical voice for a moment, and write down all the ideas you can come up with.

Record every idea that comes to you without judgment or bias. There will come a time when you will sieve through the ideas and only save the useful ones, but for this initial stage, record absolutely everything. Remem-

ber that there is no right or wrong way to record your thoughts. Some people prefer to use sticky notes, while others use audio recorders. Use whatever works for you, so long as it serves its purpose.

WRITE YOUR WORRIES

The way you handle criticism depends largely on where it originates. So, write down your criticisms, and free your mind of all lingering thoughts. Not just the ideas that come to you, but your criticisms of those ideas, too. Why do you think a particular idea might be faulty? Why do you think it just won't work? Writing these thoughts will certainly help you to gain a deeper insight into your work, as you will be able to see where corrections can be made.

FILTER

After gathering your ideas and criticisms, it is time to sift through everything. Your standard for filtering these ideas depends on many things, your personal values amongst them. Remember to set aside the ideas that don't work rather than completely discard them. Now just may not be the right time for a particular idea.

How you treat your assumptions will determine how they affect you. If you treat them as the core of all you are doing, doubts may start to set in. However, if you only use them in certain situations, where they help more than hinder, they will be a valuable tool in your belt or perhaps even a weapon in your arsenal.

DANIEL MADISON: FISHING FOR CREATIVITY

*D*aniel is a very close friend of mine and one of the most acclaimed magicians in the underground of our community. He has a unique way of branding himself as something larger than life. Daniel's contributions to the magic world are far too many and extravagant to list here, but he has written multiple best-selling books that feature his incredibly innovative and creative effects, and he has worked with just about every well-known magician of the twenty-first century. I have looked to Daniel and his work for many years as an example of what it means to be yourself and not give a shit about what anyone else thinks.

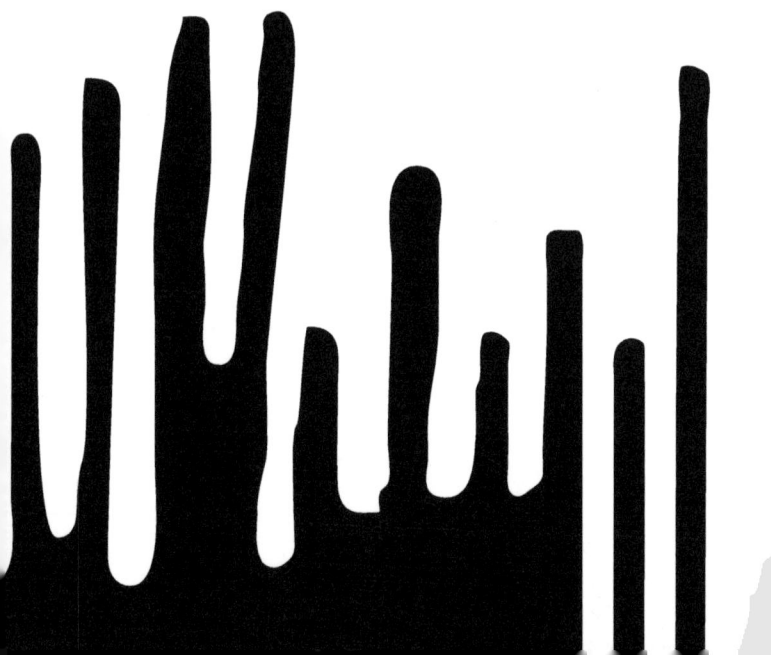

"I believe that although creativity is in us all, some of us have easier access to it. For the less creative amongst us, it's not that it's difficult to access; it's more that it's difficult to understand how to do so. I believe that anybody can decide at any moment to be creative without forcing it, but this requires that the individual knows how creativity works. The key is that one doesn't have to force it or at times even try.

I can't think of many things more unsatisfying than fishing, but nonetheless, I will use it as an analogy. A man doesn't jump into the water and swim after the fish; he doesn't try to catch the fish. Instead, he uses a technique that means the fish will come to him. All he has to do is relax and wait for the bite. Without the fishing line, he is just a man by water. We can always be that man by the water as we're always a second away from creativity—we just have

to understand how to drop that line in to initiate the session.

There is a fine line between fishing and sitting by the water like an idiot. Certain places will evoke your creativity more than others. The more comfortable and settled you are in one area, the more closed your mind will be, as it doesn't need to register or even be aware of its surroundings. Being in new places outside of your comfort zone forces your mind to open up more and take everything in. Putting yourself in situations like this means you can take advantage of the way your mind is working, so when you begin to think of new plots or effects, you have a secure line into a potentially solid creative flow; your mind is open, more aware than usual, and very susceptible to new things.

I don't think it's fair or right to suggest there is a format or a model to creativity—

there are no rules and barely any structure. If you're a card worker, you'll naturally think easier with cards as the subject. I never sit down to create, as I've learned from experience that the best and most powerful ideas have always found their way to me. This is because I'm always open to ideas. I'm not always looking or thinking, but I have just found a way to secure that line so I am always that man sitting by the water and that line is always there.

It's not easy for me to tell you how to create or even offer advice. You won't think the same as I do, and I don't think the same way you do. Nobody can tell you how you work best. That's something you will discover through trials and experimentation, and it is one of the greatest things about what we do. I stay away from magic books and DVDs and barely spend time with magicians, as I do what I can to

protect the way I'm influenced. It's the outside world and the spectators that dictate how powerful my ideas are. I don't want that to be the main point of these words, so I'll end short on one point I always live by: magic is dead. It's for you to convince your audience otherwise, no matter how big of an idea you want to find.

Don't hunt.
Go fishing.

BRAINSTORM

*S*ince we're constantly watching out for ourselves and trying to steer clear of failure and ridicule as much as possible, we effectively place ourselves into boxes that shouldn't even exist in the landscape of our lives.

When we think and have the "ah-ha" moment when an idea hits a home run, we find ourselves second-guessing after the initial excitement wears off. We say things like, "Who do I think I'm fooling? Of course, it's not good enough!" or "Maybe it isn't such a good idea after all."

In a way, you could say we prepare for failure before it even comes because greater portions of our minds expect to be and are afraid of being unprepared for it.

This is a creativity killer. You can't keep second-guessing yourself every step of the way. So, generate loads of ideas. Don't try to edit them in your head. Why? Your head is the one thing you have complete control over. At least there, you should be able to stay true to self. The mind is a powerful force, the extent of which most of us never get to know in a lifetime. When you allow your ideas to flow naturally, your mind makes connections it otherwise wouldn't have and makes sense of what seems like utter nonsense.

It's important to be in the right frame of mind to brainstorm. In today's fast-paced world of technology, distractions abound from social media, emails, SMS, and calls. These keep your mind occupied so you don't have the time and space for anything else. Find a quiet space you can exist in and limit your distractions. Place your phone on silent mode and disconnect from social media. When you do this, the ideas will swarm to you in different forms. Write down as many ideas as come to you. Don't think about what makes sense or what doesn't; write them all down the way they come to you without editing or even reading through what you wrote at the time. Trust in the spectacular power of your mind. There will be plenty of time later to edit.

After putting pen to paper and breathing life into the things in your head, mind map these ideas together and see what connections you derive from them. Treat this as a fun, silly exercise, and don't take yourself too seriously so you're able to keep the playful mindset that enhances creativity.

It's not easy, and I won't attempt to sugarcoat things. What I can tell you is that it does get easier with time. Humans are highly adaptive,

and your brain will learn the things you're interested in and those you aren't. The more you engage your mind and draw mind maps, the better you'll become at it, and when you see it working, you want more chances to play with it. Overall, you'll be getting more done and allowing your creative soul greater freedom.

VISUALIZE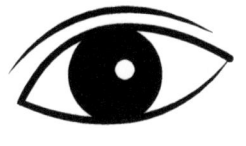

*I*deas are abstract, lifeless things. After a while with proper work, they become something tangible that can be of use to others.

When you have an idea, visualize it working or being implemented. You'll be able to discover new things about your idea. You'll be faced with the components of it that will work, those that will require a little tweaking before they do, and those you need to get rid of.

Do you see what is happening here? Your idea is getting refined; you're chipping off the unnecessary edges and maximizing the necessary ones so that, ultimately, the finished product is the very best it can be. In doing this, be optimistic, but practical. Don't set out to see the bad in every part of your idea, but don't be so optimistic that you ignore warning signs.

At this stage, you need a time and space that is all yours where you won't be disturbed. Imagine trying to engage with yourself when people are constantly in and out the door asking you numerous questions. Find a quiet place, empty your mind, and then pick an idea. When you pick that idea, ruminate on it; strip it bare and try to see everything about it in action. What are the pros? What are the cons? What are the strong points that make it better than other ideas? What are its undesirable traits? What problems will come up? Can you handle them? What possible ways can those problems be resolved? What parts of the idea will completely blow people away, and what parts will require more work?

Make notes about everything during this process. Notes are tangible evidence you can reflect on at a later date. They will give you insights into decisions you make and help you streamline them in order to make better informed ones.

Are you tired yet? The process of visualization is a very involved one; it isn't a walk in the park. It will tax you and leave you drained, but it will also provide a clearer picture of what needs to be done.

JOHN GUASTAFERRO: THE DISCIPLINE OF CREATIVITY

John Guastaferro is a magician, speaker, and member of the world-famous Magic Castle. He's a good friend who has shown me how to make my magic more impactful and emotionally appealing to my audience. I respect his work and his character immensely! John believes magic is much more than just finding a card or deceiving the senses. It's about connecting with people.

"I can't remember a time I've ever sat down and said, "Okay, today I'm going to be creative." It's something that comes about, often at unexpected moments, spawned by outside triggers and bursts of insight. I agree with Jay Sankey's comment that "creativity is something that happens more than something we actually do."

So, can we force creativity? Not exactly, but I believe we can make ourselves more attuned to opportunities that expand our thinking. By definition, creativity is aligned with fostering ideas that are new and different. Yet, one of the strongest ways to get there is to study old ideas and be as familiar as possible with the ideas of others. Use the insight gained from reading books and sessions with other magicians as a launch pad for further exploration. The freedom of creativity requires the discipline of study, research, and exploration.

In my book Discoveries & Deceptions, I talk about the importance of being constantly curious. This involves deep interest beyond our magic library and being open to learning opportunities that appear every day in the world around us. I make it a point to write down something new I've learned every day. It could be something I hear in a conversation, see on a billboard, read on a Twitter feed, or discover in any number of other sources. Try it. Download an app that allows daily entries, and make the commitment to write down at least one new thing you've learned each day.

Be a sponge for ideas that occur both inside and outside your interest in magic. This helps provide fertile ground for new discoveries. By the way, these new ideas need not be as grandiose as medical breakthroughs or archaeological finds. New ideas can come from combining concepts in different ways, applying an unlikely premise to a classic effect, or maximizing the inherent qualities of an everyday item. Often times, a simple shift in thinking can create a massive impact, an approach I talk about in my book One Degree.

Let's look at some examples.

Take my effect Lost & Found, where a card vanishes and reappears inside a clear plastic sleeve. The effect was born out of previous knowledge of Roy Walton's effect Jefferson's Jest (and related effects by Steve Hamilton and Peter Duffie). All these effects focused on vanishing a card from a clear sleeve, and I set out to discover a way to make the card reappear back inside. Using the natural friction of the plastic sleeve next to a playing card made this illusion possible.

My effect Truth in Advertising evolved by adding a small change

to my previous effect Optical Opener. The simple addition of an odd-backed card not only elevated the magic, but it also led to the advertising hook. I suppose another personal example of creativity can be found in one of my recent effects, Multi-Mental. Armed with years of exploring and performing an array of multiple-selection-type routines, I became inspired to add newness, not to the productions themselves, but to the premise—in this case, one of mindreading.

In one final example, my use of wine glasses in Vino Aces (from One Degree) came about by trying to solve a problem — in this case, trying to make MacDonald's Aces accessible to a wider audience. While the idea of using a wine goblet with playing cards dates back many years, it's application with

MacDonald's Aces was new. This also led to the creative pattern focused on the magic of toasting/clinking glasses, etc.

Creativity evolves out of the discipline of researching, questioning, seeking opportunities, solving a problem, applying previous knowledge, or striving to make your magic more personal. This is a great start for anyone wanting to be more creative. Do you always strike gold? Hardly. But the process of exploration is worth it.

Finally, don't let long periods of creative block deter you. Take enjoyment in jotting down new learnings every day, especially those that come from sources outside of magic. I think you'll find your magic becoming stronger in unexpected ways. "

FINALIZE

You have the idea. You have spent the time thinking about it, challenging it, and now you're ready to pull it all together. You now have a tangible product, something on which you can put your stamp of approval.

Life offers so many different facets; so often when we become trapped in our own world, we lose sight of what our ideal goal really is. Take a step back, and allow what you have created to percolate. During this time, you can read a book that speaks to you, listen to a talk show host who inspires you, take a walk in the gardens, or go for a soak in a hot spring.

This isn't to say you should just leave the work sitting there gathering dust without doing anything about it. If you do that, you might lose the momentum that has taken you such time and effort to build, and you could even lose some of the finer aspects of your idea. Leave it for a day or two, and after clearing your mind, you can then revisit all the notes you made during your brainstorming and visualization sessions. Then, you can put together the things that work into a new list, from which you can begin to wrap up all the loose ends of your idea.

This stage of organizing is meant to help consolidate and streamline your ideas.

When you do this, it won't be smooth sailing. It will be tough, and sometimes, you'll want to give up. But if you fall underneath the weight of it all, you'll have lost more than just your idea. You will have lost your time, energy, your brain power, and conviction. You will have let down that relentless voice inside your head that continuously tells you to go for it.

So, in putting it all together, know there are battles you will have to fight, and a lot of them you will feel ill-equipped for. Fight all the obstacles in your path. Know that, like failures, they, too, are brimming with valuable lessons that can aid you in the process of bringing your new idea to life.

CONCLUDING RITES:

*H*ey, you've made it this far. Congratulations! More than anything else, I want you to realize you are creative. I want you to live your most fulfilled, passionate life and to follow your creativity, whatever it may be. If we all focus on creativity—if, like a tidal wave, millions of people realize that they're creative, and they then use that creativity to impact the world around them positively—we will change the world for the better.

Is that a lofty goal? Sure thing. But a possible one? Most definitely. Every decision we make impacts others. If we choose to use our creativity to fuel the world in which we live and forego the fear, doubt, and self-destruction that attempt to inhibit us from creation, then we can create the lives we want to lead and cultivate the kind of world we want to live in.

This is the mission; the next steps are up to you. It's time for you to accept the challenge of living a creative life. You're the only one who can follow through on unearthing your own creativity, and so in that vein, I have crafted a 30-Day Creativity Challenge, in which I take you through all the necessary steps to truly implement creativity in your life.

All you have to do is check in each day with the workbook I've created for the challenge, complete a creative exercise or two, and absorb a trick, tip, or piece of advice. Checking in with the morning routine and creativity exercises will push you forward in expressing your creativity, living your creative life, and leaving your stamp on the earth.

When we are dead and gone, the only thing that remains of us is what we've created. I have had the gift of creating two beautiful children. They are part of my creativity; I created these amazing things that move, emote, and express, all on their own. In raising them, I've encouraged them to adopt a mindset that will hopefully carry on my legacy of creative expression. But this legacy can be left in any way you see fit. So please go out there, and carry these ideas and ideals of creativity in action onward.

Live the most creative life you can, starting with the 30-Day Creativity Challenge, found within this book.

GRATITUDE

I would like to start by expressing gratitude to my mother and father. Without their support, I never would have built up the confidence to express myself so freely.

To all my friends in the magic community, I'd like to say thank you for the support you have shown me and my creations over the years. You all play a huge part in who I am, and for that you have my deepest respect.

I am extremely grateful to everyone who helped make this book a reality: everyone who contributed to the essays within, to all the readers who sent me their constructive criticism, and every other hand that helped me turn an idea into what you're now holding in your hands.

Lastly, I am grateful for my beautiful wife Natasha and our two perfect children, Carter and Alina. You are the reason for everything I create. I still ask God every day what I did to deserve such a beautiful family.

ABOUT THE AUTHOR:

*W*hen Adam was six years old, he showed his first magic trick to his father and, at that moment, knew this was what he wanted to do for the rest of his life. The look of wonder and joy on his dad's face triggered something in Adam that made him know, even at such a young age, he was born to create and perform magic.

Devoting not just his childhood, but his entire life, to the art of magic, Adam has become the general manager of the most successful magic store of all time, Ellusionist, and has gone on to invent many products, including various magic tricks, decks of playing cards, and illusions that are used by fellow magicians all over the world—including his most recent invention, the Fiddle stick. Adam has invented some of the best-selling magic tricks of all time.

Adam currently lives in New Hampshire with his wife Natasha and their two children, Carter and Alina. He performs his keynote speech on creativity and award-winning magic and mind reading shows all over the world. While not performing, he spends his time inventing viral products and innovative magic tricks and illusions.

TAKE A MINUTE TO PAT
YOURSELF ON THE BACK

As with the creative process, beginning something is the easy part, finishing it is what separates the winners from the drifters. The last part of this book is simply to get you inspired. I've researched some inventions that have interesting stories about the creative process. There is no easy path to something beautiful. Even things as simple as Potato Chips have a very unique and insightful creative process behind them.

I hope this last section inspires you to hold nothing back in your creative adventures. Sometimes the goofiest idea that was given the right amount of love and attention becomes the most impressive piece once it's brought to life.

AWESOME INVENTIONS

POTATO CHIPS

*T*hey have been one of our favorite snacks from the time we were kids, right through adulthood. However, do you know how these crispy delicious treats were invented? It has been said that they were actually part of a little revenge plot. Hotel chef George Crum enjoyed a wonderful knack for cooking. From his kitchen at Moon's Lake House near Saratoga Springs, N.Y., Mr. Crum could "take anything edible and transform it into a dish fit for a king." That skill came in handy – the upscale Lake House attracted customers who were used to being treated like kings. In 1853, a cranky guest complained about Crum's fried potatoes.

They were too thick, he said. Too soggy and bland. The patron demanded a new batch. Crum did not take this well. He decided to play a trick on the diner. The chef sliced a potato paper-thin, fried it until a fork could shatter the thing, and then purposefully over-salted his new creation. The persnickety guest will hate this, he thought. However, the plan backfired. The person loved it! He ordered a second serving. Word of this new snack spread quickly. "Saratoga Chips" became a hit across New England, and Crum went on to open his own restaurant. Today, that accidental invention has ballooned into a massive snack industry.

X-RAYS

*I*n the late 1800s, the world became a seemingly magical place. Scientists discovered radiation, radio waves, and other invisible forces of nature. For a while there, many serious researchers joined séances and believed in ghosts. Science had discovered so many mysterious phenomena – things that the eye could not see but were definitely there – that many people wondered, what else might be out there?

German physicist Wilhelm Röntgen discovered one of these invisible powers by accident. Röntgen experimented with cathode-ray tubes, which are glass tubes with the air sucked out and a special gas pumped in them. They work like modern-day fluorescent light bulbs. When Röntgen ran electricity through the gas, the tube would glow. However, something strange happened after he surrounded the tube with black cardboard. When he turned on the machine, a chemical a few feet away started to glow. The cardboard should have prevented any light from escaping, so what caused this distant glow?

Little did he know that the cathode-ray tube had been sending out more than just visible light. It shot out invisible rays that could pass right through paper, wood, and even skin. The lab chemical that lit up – the one that tipped off Röntgen – reacted to these rays. He called the phenomenon X-rays. The X stood for "unknown."

He continued his experiments using photographic plate to capture the image of various objects of random thickness placed in the path of the rays. He generated the very first "roentgenogram" by developing the image of his wife's hand and analyzed the variable transparency as showed by her bones, flesh and her wedding ring. Upon seeing this skeletal image, she exclaimed, "I have seen my own death!". Based on his subsequent research and experiments, he declared that X-ray beams are produced by the impact of cathode rays on material objects.

STAINLESS STEEL

Steel has been forged for millennia, with the earliest known examples reaching back to Turkey in the 18th century BC.

Steel, which is iron with a small amount of carbon added to it, offers some advantages over iron in terms of hardness, ductility, and tensile strength, but because it is still mostly iron, it rusts. Everything made out of steel will, over time, inexorably transform into a crumbling powder. Throughout the ages, metallurgists attempted to add other elements to steel to prevent rusting, sometimes with modest success. But there was no reliable way of mass-producing rustproof steel until 1912, when a metallurgist named Harry Brearly from the English city of Sheffield tried to come up with a better gun. Most gun barrels are grooved or "rifled" in a spiral pattern that causes the bullet to spin, increasing accuracy. However, the friction between the bullet and the barrel causes wear, eventually making the barrel too big for the bullet. Brearly sought to develop a steel alloy that would resist erosion.

He failed multiple times, and his heap of steel scraps grew bigger and bigger. After several months of trying and failing, Brearly noticed that one of his failures had retained its luster, while the others had rusted. The sample contained about 12 percent chromium, which had reacted with the oxygen in the air to form a thin, protective film. Even when it was scratched, the film would quickly restore itself. Brearly called his invention "rust-less steel."

Since the 16th century, Brearly's hometown of Sheffield was known for manufacturing cutlery, and Brearly immediately saw the potential for his new invention. Up until then, most cutlery was made of ordinary steel, which had to be polished frequently to avoid rusting, or silver, which was prohibitively expensive for many people. Brearly approached his old schoolmate Ernest Stuart, who was a manager at Mosley's Portland Works. After testing Brearly's material in a vinegar solution, he dubbed it "stainless steel," and the name stuck. The Portland Works building still stands in Sheffield, where it serves as a low-cost space for independent cutlery makers and metallurgists, along with many artists and musicians.

PLASTIC

Chances are that, right now, you can spot a half dozen plastic items without even having to turn your head. In fact, if you are wearing glasses with lightweight or scratch-resistant lenses, chances are that everything you see is, in a sense, plastic-wrapped. Leo Baekeland, the Belgian-born chemist who in 1907 developed the first plastic, probably did not set out to dominate your visual field with his creation. His original goal was much more modest: to find a replacement for shellac, a resin secreted by a South Asian scale bug.

Baekeland's "Novolak," a combination of formaldehyde and phenol – an acid extracted from coal tar – failed to catch on as a shellac substitute. Little did he know he was about to stumble on something far more important. But he noticed that by controlling the temperature and pressure applied to the two compounds (using a massive iron cooker that he called a bakelizer) and by mixing it with wood flour, asbestos, or slate dust, he had created a material that was moldable yet robust as well as non-conductive and heat-resistant. He dubbed his invention Bakelite, and referred to it as "the material of 1,000 uses."

He underestimated its potential by several orders of magnitude. In the following decades, Bakelite was used to make electronics components, auto parts, cameras, telephones, buttons, letter openers, clocks, radios, toys, telephone casings, billiard balls, kitchenware, rosary beads, chess pieces, and tens of thousands of other items. Over the 20th century, Bakelite and its descendants – Plexiglas, polyester, vinyl, nylon, polyurethane, polycarbonate, and so on – transformed the stuff that our world is made of, from natural to synthetic. Items that were crafted from wood, ivory, or marble, are now affordable for almost everyone. Yet at the same time, the ersatz topography that Baekeland brought forth does not always sit easily with us. What's more, most petroleum-derived plastics will remain in the environment for centuries, if not millennia.

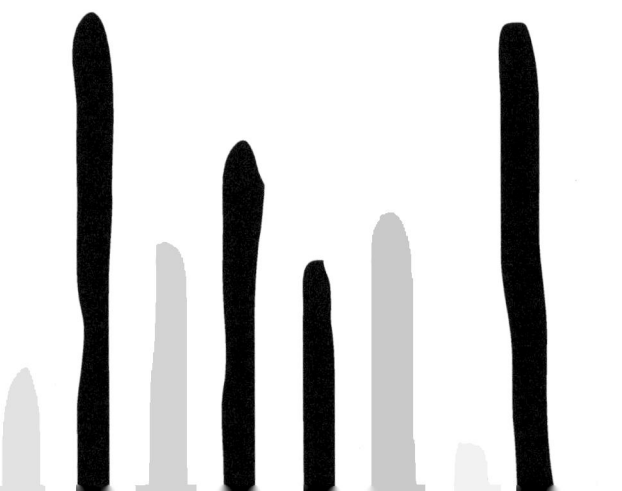

SACCHARIN

Saccharin came as a sweet surprise (Pun Intended). Before Sweet'N Low and diet sodas, there was a plucky researcher studying something completely different: coal tar. In the 1870s, Russian chemist Constantin Fahlberg worked in the lab of Ira Remsen at Johns Hopkins University. Remsen's team experimented with coal-tar derivatives, seeing how they react to phosphorus, chloride, ammonia, and other chemicals. (Not exactly the most appetizing profession). One night, Fahlberg returned home and started to chow down on dinner rolls. Something was off. The rolls tasted curiously sweet. The recipe had not changed, so what was going on here? He soon realized that it was not the rolls. It was him. His hands were covered with a mystery chemical that made everything sweet.

"Fahlberg had literally brought his work home with him, having spilled an experimental compound over his hands earlier that day," writes the Chemical Heritage Foundation in its history of saccharin. "He ran back to Remsen's laboratory, where he tasted everything on his worktable—all the vials, beakers, and dishes he used for his experiments. Finally he found the source: an over boiled beaker". Fahlberg had actually created saccharin before, but since he never bothered to taste-test his concoctions, the chemist had no idea. In fact, a modern chemist probably would have never discovered saccharin. Nowadays, people thoroughly wash their hands before leaving the lab. If Fahlberg had followed the normal rules of cleanliness, the world would be without this zero-calorie artificial sweetener.

TEFLON

𝓡oy Plunkett invented Teflon while trying to make a better refrigerator. When the DuPont chemist was only 27 years old, he had a big idea. Plunkett wanted to combine a specific gas with hydrochloric acid. He gathered the desired gas (tetrafluoroethylene) but wasn't quite ready to start experimenting. So he cooled and pressurized the gas in canisters overnight. But when he returned the next day, the gas was gone. The canisters weighed the same amount as when they were full, but nothing came out. Where did all the gas go?

Confused, Plunkett cut the canisters in half. The gas had solidified on the sides, creating a slick surface.

"Rather than discard the apparent mistake, Plunkett and his assistant tested the new polymer and found that it had some very unusual properties: it was extremely slippery as well as inert to virtually all chemicals, including highly corrosive acids," writes DuPont in its corporate history. "The product, trademarked as Teflon in 1945, was first used by the military in artillery shell fuses and in the production of nuclear material for the Manhattan Project." While Plunkett invented Teflon, he didn't come up with the idea of using it for cooking. About a decade after Plunkett sawed those canisters in half, a French engineer named Marc Grégoire introduced "Tefal" pans, the first to be lined in Teflon. The idea came from his wife. Before Tefal, Grégoire used Teflon on his fishing tackle to prevent tangling. But his wife realized that the nonstick surface would be perfect for cookware.

PLAY-DOH

*T*he modeling "Doh," with the unique smell, that children (and even adults) love to play with was not originally used for fun and games. In fact, it was used for the exact opposite: cleaning.

Before World War II, coal was commonly used to heat homes, which left soot stains on walls. Noah and Joseph McVicker of Kutol Products, a Cincinnati-based soap manufacturer, created the doughy material to rub the soot off wallpaper. However, after the war, natural gas became a more common heat source. As coal was phased out, few people needed Kutol's cleaning product. The company faced bankruptcy.

In the early 1950s, Joseph McVicker learned that his sister, a schoolteacher, used the material in her classroom as modeling dough. And thus, Play-Doh was born. The McVickers decided to market their nontoxic creation as a children's toy. In 1955, they tested their product at nurseries and schools. A year later, they created the company Rainbow Crafts.

The "Play-Doh smell" came from the McVickers trying to hide the original cleaning aroma. Many ingredients of Play-Doh are not publicly known, but it is said that the McVickers added an artificial almond scent to the recipe.

In 1956, Play-Doh was first sold at Woodward and Lothrop, a department store in Washington, D.C. It came in only one color – off-white. Colored Play-Doh came out the following year and was sold at more department stores, such as Macy's in New York. The McVickers became millionaires as Play-Doh ads were broadcast on kids' shows such as "Captain Kangaroo," "Ding Dong School," and "Romper Room."

MAUVE

Chemist William Perkin wanted to cure malaria. Instead, he started a new movement in the fashion industry.

In 1856, Perkin was an 18-year-old student at the Royal College of London. He attempted to create artificial quinine, an anti-malaria drug derived from tree bark. He was unsuccessful. However, his curiosity spiked when his failures resulted in a thick, purple sludge.

The color caught his eye. The sludge, made with a carbon-rich tar from distilled coal, took on a unique shade of purple, a very popular color in the fashion world at the time. Perkin was able to isolate the compound producing the color, which he named "mauve." Perkin had created the first-ever synthetic dye.

Perkin dropped out of school and his father, George, used his entire life savings to build a factory that produced mauve-colored items. Within a few years, the family became extremely wealthy.

Perkin's dye was quite vibrant and didn't fade or wash out, but that's not the only good thing that came from Perkin's new color. Mauve helped kick-start a chemistry revolution. Experiments from other labs soon resulted in thousands of useful carbon compounds, such as an actual artificial quinine.

SUPERGLUE

*E*astman Kodak researcher Harry Coover discovered Superglue years before he figured out what to do with it. At first, its stickiness infuriated him.

Coover first came across cyanoacrylates (the chemical name for these überadhesives) in World War II. His team tried to use the material to create plastic gunsights. Too bad the cyanoacrylates kept sticking to everything. Coover dismissed the chemical and tried diferent approaches.

He came across the material again in 1951. This time, Kodak experimented with cyanoacrylates for heat-resistant jet airplane canopies. Again, the stickiness got in the way. But then Coover had an epiphany. "Coover realized these sticky adhesives had unique properties in that they required no heat or pressure to bond," writes the Massachusetts Institute of Technology (MIT) in a column from 2004. "He and his team tried the substance on various items in the lab and each time, the items became permanently bonded together. Coover – and his employer – knew they were on to something."

While Coover's original patent called the new invention "Superglue," Kodak sold the adhesive under the less-evocative name "Eastman 910." "Later it became known as Super Glue, and Coover became somewhat of a celebrity, appearing on television in the show 'I've Got a Secret,' where he lifted the host, Garry Moore, off the ground using a single drop of the substance," writes MIT.

SILLY PUTTY

You can stretch it. You can bounce it. You can throw it. The eraser-colored goo was not intended to become one of America's favorite childhood toys, but actually a synthetic substitute for rubber during World War II. Rubber – used for tires, gas masks, life rafts, and boots – was essential for the war. With Japan attacking many rubber-manufacturing countries in Asia, America was in a pickle. Citizens were asked to donate any old tires, rain boots, coats, and anything else made of rubber.

But it still wasn't enough. The government reached out to companies to invent a synthetic rubber with similar properties.

In 1943, James Wright, an engineer working for General Electric, entered the scene. Wright just happened to combine boric acid and silicone oil in one of his test tubes, creating the goo that would eventually fill hours of playtime.

The goo could rebound and stretch more than traditional rubber, had a very high melting temperature, and did not collect mold. Although the "nutty putty" didn't contain the properties needed to replace rubber,

Wright hoped there would be some conventional use for it.

However, the government was not interested. Wright sent samples of it to scientists around the country and they, too, were not interested. However, partygoers found the goo very entertaining. In 1949, a second character entered the scene: the unemployed Peter Hodgson, who saw an opportunity. He borrowed $147 to buy the rights from GE and began producing the goo, which he renamed Silly Putty. He packaged it in plastic eggs because it was close to Easter.

Soon children across the country wanted Silly Putty. Kids could stretch and distort their favorite comic book heroes by slapping the putty down on printed pages. It became one of the fastest selling toys in America's history.

CORN FLAKES

Corn Flakes were created (by accident, of course) during a search for good, wholesome vegetarian food. William Kellogg and his brother, John Kellogg, are the masterminds behind one of the world's most popular cold cereals.

In 1894, John was the chief medical officer of Battle Creek Sanitarium in Michigan, which was run based on Seventh-day Adventist health principles of a vegetarian diet. Will worked at the sanitarium as a bookkeeper and manager, but under the guidance of his brother, he became very interested in health and nutrition. He eventually helped John search for new, wholesome diets for patients. The two brothers were in search of an easily digestible bread substitute, which led them to boiling wheat to make dough.

But it never turned into dough. They let the wheat boil for far too long. When Will rolled out the wheat, it separated into large, flat flakes. After baking and tasting, the brothers decided it was a delicious, healthy snack worthy of their patients. "Granose" flakes received rave reviews and patients pleaded for more after they left the sanitarium.

While John started the shipment process, Will had an idea: Try the process with corn instead of wheat. It was a touch-down play. In 1906 alone, the Kelloggs' company, Battle Creek Toasted Corn Flakes Company, shipped 175,000 cases of Corn Flakes, according to the Massachusetts Institute of Technology.

The brothers experimented with more ingredients, creating Bran Flakes and Rice Krispies. After Will decided to add sugar to some recipes, John left the company, believing that it went against their initial goals. Will renamed the company W.K. Kellogg Company in 1922.

SLINKY

Like James Wright (inventor of Silly Putty), engineer Richard James researched to aid American troops during World War II. In his home laboratory in Philadelphia, James attempted to invent springs that would support and stabilize sensitive instruments on naval ships during rough seas. One spring was knocked off the worktable and stepped its way down to the floor.

After James watched it re-coil itself and stand upright on the floor, a light bulb went off in his brain.

James showed the stepping spring to his wife, Betty, and said he could make a children's toy out of it. Because the Navy was unresponsive to the springs, James spent the next couple of years perfecting his toy idea. Betty came up with the name "Slinky" and the couple first demonstrated its toy at Gimbels Department Store in 1945. In just 90 minutes, they sold 400 Slinkys.

Within 50 years, James Industries sold more than a quarter of a billion Slinkys worldwide and the slinking toy is still finding its way into American pop culture.

The Slinky jingle is the longest-running song in advertisement history. It first aired in 1962: What walks down stairs, alone or in pairs, and makes a slinkity sound?
A spring, a spring, a marvelous thing! Everyone knows it's Slinky.

It's Slinky, it's Slinky. For fun it's a wonderful toy. It's Slinky, it's Slinky. It's fun for a girl or a boy. It's fun for a girl or boy!

VELCRO

*M*any dog owners grumble when their loyal companions play outside and return with all sorts of nature stuck to their fur and feet, bringing the outside environment into their once-clean homes.

But not Swiss electrical engineer, George De Mestral, who, after taking a walk in the woods with his dog, was fascinated by the cockleburs' ability to cling to his clothes and his dog's fur.

Under a microscope, De Mestral examined the tons of tiny hooks that line cockleburs and discovered they could easily attach to the small loops found in clothing and fur. He experimented with different materials to make his own hooks and loops form a stronger bond. In 1955, De Mestral decided nylon was perfect and thus Velcro was invented.

Velcro, the combination of "velvet" and "crochet," was showcased in a 1959 fashion show held at the Waldorf-Astoria Hotel in New York City. However, it didn't receive positive reviews from fashion enthusiasts.

Velcro wasn't widely used until NASA made it popular in the early 1960s. Apollo astronauts used it to secure items that they didn't want escaping in their zero-gravity environment. Hospitals and athletic companies eventually used Velcro after realizing the practicality of the material. In 1968, Puma was the first to use Velcro on shoes – Adidas, Reebok, and others followed suit.

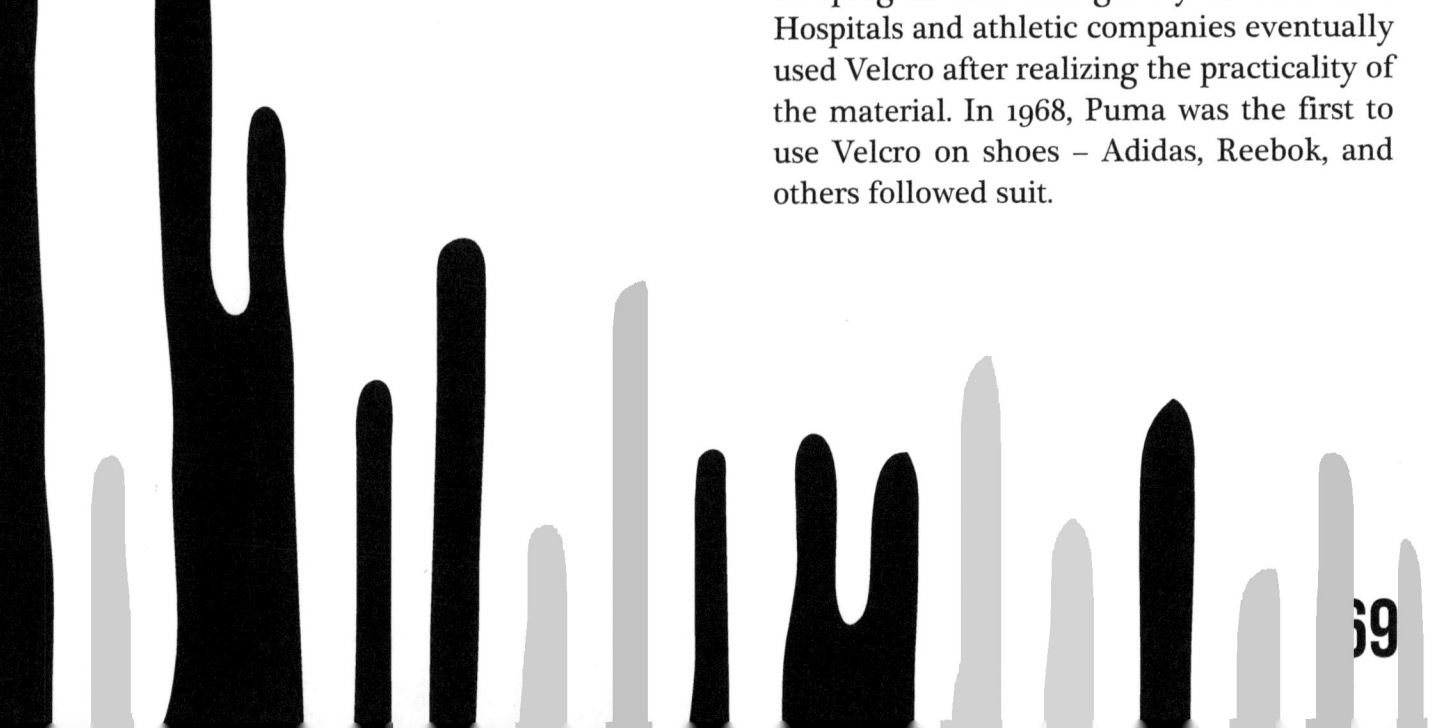

VULCANIZED RUBBER

*I*n the early 1830s, natural rubber was all the rage, but the excitement faded. People realized that their rubber would freeze and crack during the winter or melt into a sticky, smelly goo during the summer. Natural rubber could not stand extreme temperatures, so its popularity quickly died.

Charles Goodyear spent years trying to overcome rubber's problems, and he only succeeded by mistake.

Goodyear tried various powders to dry up the stickiness, but to no avail. Everything kept melting. These expensive experiments pushed his family into debt and resulted in jail time. Yet even in prison, Goodyear was undeterred from his goal. Some called him a mad man.

According to a biography of Goodyear in Reader's Digest, he walked into a general store in Woburn, Mass., to show off his rubber products. This time the rubber had sulfur in it to act as a drying agent. Goodyear got so excited that the rubber flew out of his hands and landed on a hot stove. When he examined it, he noticed that it did not melt, but instead charred black. After poking and prodding, Goodyear also noticed that it still had the springy surface texture of rubber, the "gum-elastic" it was known for. Goodyear had made rubber weatherproof.

Another tale tells a different story: Goodyear absent-mindedly turned out the lights to his makeshift lab and spilled his vials and test tubes containing sulfur, lead, and rubber onto a still-hot stove. The result was the same, a charred rubber-like substance that didn't melt in the extreme heat. After testing in freezing temperatures, Goodyear finally succeeded in reaching his goal, and it only happened because of a careless mistake.

After many patent battles, Goodyear died still in debt. He didn't start the Goodyear Tire and Rubber Co. – the American company was instead named in his honor.

"Life," Goodyear wrote, "should not be estimated exclusively by the standard of dollars and cents. I am not disposed to complain that I have planted and others have gathered the fruits. A man has cause for regret only when he sows and no one reaps."

POPSICLES

*K*ids love Popsicles, so it makes sense that an 11-year-old boy invented them.

In 1905, Frank Epperson from San Francisco invented the Popsicle purely by accident. Epperson made a fruit-flavored soda drink out of powder and water, a popular concoction back then. However, one evening, he never finished making the soda and left it outside overnight – with the stirring stick still in the cup. It was a cold night, and he discovered in the morning that the drink had frozen around the stick. He popped it out of the cup and licked it.

At first, Epperson didn't realize what he had stumbled upon. Seventeen years later, he served the frozen lollipops to the public at a fireman's ball. (Surprisingly, no one else had come up with the idea yet). They were a huge hit. A year later, he enjoyed even more success after serving them at Neptune Beach, an amusement park in Alameda, Calif., which closed in 1939.

Epperson finally applied for the patent in 1923 and began producing even more fruit flavors. He sold the frozen pops on birch wood sticks and called them "Eppsicles." They sold for just a nickel apiece. Epperson's children apparently didn't like the name "Eppsicle." They preferred "Popsicles." Epperson eventually agreed with his kids, and the name has stuck ever since.

CHOCOLATE CHIP COOKIES

*I*f your favorite cookie is chocolate chip, then you should praise Ruth Graves Wakefield for her mistakes in the kitchen.

Wakefield and her husband, Kenneth, owned Toll House Inn in Whitman, Mass. Wakefield prepared the recipes and cooked for the inn's guests.

One day in 1930, Wakefield had a problem. She was out of baker's chocolate for her scrumptious Butter Drop Do cookies. Surely, her guests would be upset. Wakefield had to quickly come up with a chocolate substitute and broke up a bar of Nestle's semisweet chocolate into tiny chunks and mixed them into the batter. She assumed that the chocolate would melt, spread into the dough as it baked, and create a chocolate-flavored cookie.

That, of course, didn't happen. When Wakefield took the cookies out of the oven, she noticed that the chocolate chunks only melted slightly, holding their shape and forming a creamy texture. The guests loved them.

Wakefield's chocolate chip cookies began attracting people from all over New England. After her recipe appeared in a Boston newspaper, Nestle gained a huge spike in sales. Everyone wanted Nestle's semisweet chocolate bars to make Wakefield's cookies.

Therefore, a marketing deal was struck. Andrew Nestle agreed to give Wakefield a lifetime supply of the chocolate in return for her recipe printed on every Nestle semisweet chocolate bar.

MICROWAVE OVEN

*I*t started out more than five feet tall, weighed 750 pounds, and cost about $5,000. The first microwave, the Radarange, built by Raytheon Corporation in 1947, was based on the accidental discovery of a melted chocolate bar.

Several years prior to Raytheon's first attempt at the microwave oven, a scientist, Percy Spencer, experimented with a new magnetron, a vacuum tube that releases energy to power radar equipment.
Radar was vital during World War II. It allowed for easier detection of enemy planes and ships, especially German U-Boats. Raytheon scientists looked for new ways to improve the magnetron and increase productivity during a time of great need.

Cooking a TV dinner was not on their to-do lists. It was only by chance – and after the war had ended – that one scientist finally noticed one of the magnetron's other possible uses.

While working with the device, Spencer noticed that the chocolate bar in his pocket started melting. He attributed it to the microwaves and, like any good scientist, conducted more tests.

First, Spencer tried corn kernels. After they successfully popped, Spencer tried heating more foods. The results led engineers to attempt to contain the microwaves in a safe enclosure, the microwave oven. The Amana Corporation (acquired by Raytheon in 1965) first introduced the countertop microwave oven that is in almost all American kitchens today to the public in 1967.

THE ICE-CREAM CONE

The invention of the actual ice cream cone, or "cornet," still remains a controversial mystery. But what is widely accepted is the cone-shaped edible ice cream holder was indeed an accident.

In the late 1800s and early 1900s, ice cream prices dropped and the creamy dessert quickly became a more popular treat. Ice cream street vendors popped up across the US and in Europe. The competition was over more than just flavors; it came down to what they put the ice cream in.

Paper, glass, and metal were common materials used for holding ice cream. Then came the not so sanitary "penny licks." Many vendors would scoop their flavor of the day into a glass and hungry buyers would pay a penny to lick the glass clean before returning it to the vender. Not only was this not the cleanest way to eat dessert, but also customers kept breaking the glass or "accidentally" walking away with them.

In 1902, Antonio Valvona filed the first patent in Britain for an edible ice cream cup. The second came from Italo Marchiony, an Italian immigrant living in New York. However, these patents covered bowl, not cones.

So where did the cone-shaped ice cream holder come from? Historians agree on the "where" and "when," but not the "who."

The 1904 World's Fair in St. Louis celebrated the centennial of the Louisiana Purchase (though one year late). The food was plentiful, and historians say there were more than 50 ice cream venders and over a dozen waffle stands. With the heat, ice cream was the top seller – hot waffles not so much.

But the waffles proved useful when all the ice cream venders ran out of cups.

The generally accepted story goes likes this: ice cream vender Arnold Fornachou couldn't keep up with demand and ran out of paper dishes. Ernest Hamwi, a vender next to Mr. Fornachou sold "zalabia," a waffle-like pastry. Because his zalabia wasn't selling, Mr. Hamwi decided to help his neighbor by rolling up one of his waffle pastries and giving it to Fornachou who put ice cream in it. Viola, the first ice cream cone sold.

Other venders teamed up as well, each claiming that it invented the idea. With all the hustle and bustle of the World's Fair, no one really knows who invented the cone first. Many patents were filed after the fair for "waffle-rolling" machines, but many still take the credit for this accidental invention.

POST-IT NOTES

*T*hey come in all colors of the rainbow, but the original came in only yellow – and that too was an accident. Post-it Notes are now a must-have tool for many offices, but they wouldn't exist without a chemical engineer, a church choir singer, and a persistent laboratory manager.

It all started with Spencer Silver, a chemist for 3M, a large manufacturing company. In 1968, Mr. Spencer was supposed to be inventing a strong adhesive for the aerospace industry. However, he accidentally made the exact opposite: a weak adhesive made of tiny acrylic microspheres.

The spheres were nearly indestructible and would stick well even after several uses. At first, 3M considered Spencer's invention useless.

Spencer wanted to sell the adhesive as a sticky surface for bulletin boards. He imagined people attaching notes to the board and peeling them off when they were done – no nails or tacks required. The idea didn't catch on.

Five years later, Art Fry – another 3M chemist and frequent choir singer – invented the Post-it Note in a moment of extreme frustration.

All of Mr. Fry's paper bookmarks kept falling out! Every time he stood and opened his hymnal, the small slips of paper would disappear into the book or fall to the floor. Fry needed a way to open his hymnal right to the page, without the messy hassle.

Fry had an idea: Instead of putting the adhesive on a bulletin board, put it on the paper. That way, you could stick the paper on anything. He took his idea to Spencer, who of course was ecstatic. The higher-ups at 3M still weren't. The product was put on the back burner for another three years.

Fortunately, a laboratory manager named Geoff Nicholson believed in the idea. Mr. Nicholson decided that if 3M's marketing department wouldn't back the product, then his lab team would market it themselves. They handed out free samples and 90 percent of the people ordered more Post-it Notes.

Fun fact: According to Nicholson, the standard Post-its are yellow because they first used yellow scrap paper from the lab next door. When they ran out of scrap, they just bought more yellow paper. No one thought to change the color ... yet.

MATCHES

*F*or more than 100,000 years, humans have been playing with fire. But no one could create a really easy way to start a fire until a British pharmacist tried to clean his stirring utensil. In 1826, John Walker was stirring a pot of chemicals when he noticed a dried lump had formed on the end of the mixing stick. Without thinking, he tried to scrape off the dried gob and – all of a sudden – it ignited.

Mr. Walker sold the first strikeable matches at a local bookstore. The "friction lights" were three inches long and came neatly in a box with a piece of sandpaper.

Walker wasn't interested in patenting the idea, so Samuel Jones copied the matches and sold "Lucifers." They were a little more practical than Walker's friction lights. Lucifers were shorter and came in a smaller cardboard box for easy carrying. The earliest description of a match-like product appears in a Chinese book titled "Records of the Unworldly and the Strange," by Tao Gu, circa 950 AD. They were called "fire-inch sticks" and used sulfur to start the flame. Still, they were not strike able.

first self-igniting match in 1805. Mr. Chancel's method involved a wooden splint tipped with sugar and potassium chlorate that was carefully dipped into a small bottle of concentrated sulfuric acid.

Chancel's method was highly unpleasant and dangerous. The mix of chemicals produced a yellow smelly gas called chlorine dioxide, which explodes when it comes into contact with pretty much anything.

Today, matches are made with non-poisonous red phosphorus, discovered by Johan Edvard Lundstrom. The Diamond Match Company was the first to sell "safety matches" in the US, forfeiting their patent rights to allow all match companies to produce safe matches.

SAFETY GLASS

Back in the early days of automobiles, before seatbelts and airbags were part of the package, one of the gravest dangers was injury from shards of shattered windshield glass. We can thank French artist and chemist Édouard Bénédictus for chancing upon the invention of laminated glass, also known as safety glass. While in his lab, a glass flask dropped and broke but didn't shatter, Bénédictus realized that the interior was coated with plastic cellulose nitrate that held the now-harmless broken pieces together. He applied for a patent in 1909 with a vision of increasing the safety of cars, but manufacturers rejected the idea to keep costs down. However, the glass became standard for gas mask lenses in World War I. With its success on the battlefield, the automobile industry finally ceded and by the 1930s, most cars were equipped with glass that didn't splinter into jagged pieces upon impact.

VIAGRA

*M*uch like the fountain of youth, humans have long sought magic ingredients that promise to boost the libido and enhance sexual function. But the breakthrough that gave us Viagra (sildenafil) didn't occur when researchers were looking for ways to make men manly; rather, they were testing sildenafil as a cure for hypertension and heart disease. After two phases of testing, researchers concluded that the drug failed to show promising results for the heart, but test subjects noted that … well, you know what part of the body it did wonders for. Bingo! Pfizer patented Viagra in 1996 and the U.S. FDA approved it for use in erectile dysfunction in 1998. Sales of Viagra continue to exceed well more than $1 billion per year. Bonus tip: Researchers have also found that 1 milligram of sildenafil dissolved in a vase of water can make fresh cut flowers, um, "stand at attention" for up to a week beyond their natural life span.

SMART DUST

*A*s part of her doctoral project, Jamie Link was working on a silicon chip when BANG! – it suddenly shattered into myriad tiny pieces. Game over? Not for this chemist. Blessed with an open and inquiring mind, Link simply shifted her scientific gaze. What she soon discovered was that her newly created smart dust retained the properties of the original chip and could still function as programmable sensors.

Give the silicon particles a target to aim at and they'll not only seek it out, but join together and change color when they find it. As for the target – and here's the exciting bit – it could be anything from deadly tumor cells in the body to toxic chemicals carried in the air or water. Now that's a welcome mistake.

SCOTCHGARD

*I*nventor: Patsy Sherman, a chemist for 3M. What she was trying to make: In 1953, Sherman was assigned to work on a project to develop a rubber material that would not deteriorate from exposure to jet aircraft fuels. How it was created: An assistant accidentally dropped the mixture Sherman was experimenting with on her shoe. While the rest of her shoe became dirty and stained, one spot remained bright and clean. She retraced her steps and identified the stain resistant compound, known today as Scotchguard.

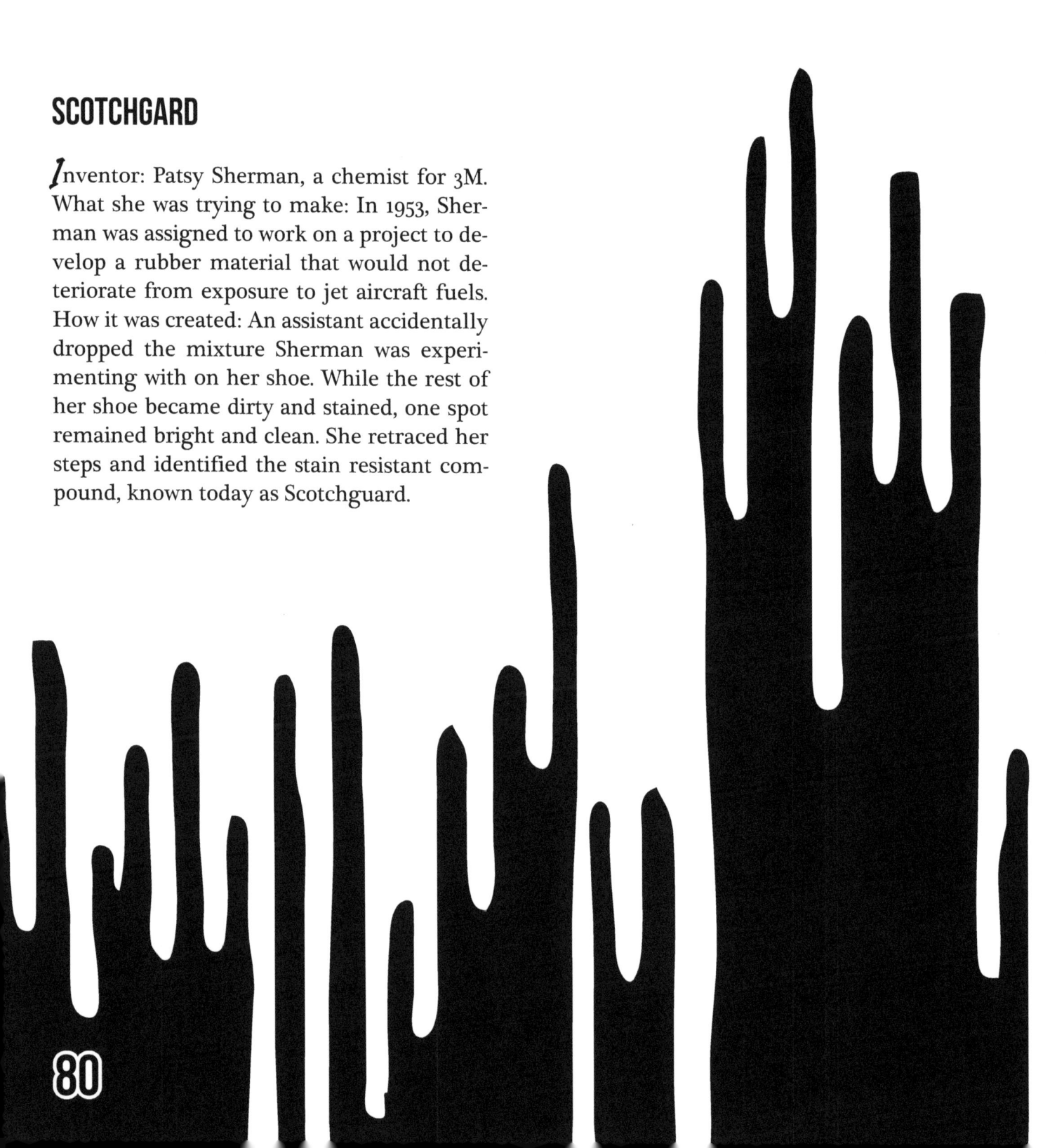

THE PACEMAKER

*I*n the 1950s, Greatbatch had left the Navy and was working as medical researcher. He was building an oscillator to record heart sounds when he pulled the wrong resistor out of a box. When he assembled his device, it began to give off a rhythmic electrical pulse. It was then he realized his invention could be used as a pacemaker. He spent two years refining his device and was awarded a patent for world's first implantable pacemaker.

Before then, pacemakers were the size of a TV and shocked patients during use, so you can imagine how an implantable device would change people's lives. His first pacemaker was implanted in a 77-year-old patient who lived 18 months with the device. In 1985, the National Society of Professional Engineers recognized his pacemaker as one of the ten greatest engineering achievements of the last 50 years.

Sources: rd.com, todayifoundout.com, mentalfloss. com, medicaldaily.com, macleans.ca, medicinenet. com, acs.org, lemelson.mit.edu, chemheritage.org, live-science.com, kotexfits.com, menstrualcup.co, modern-notion.com, deathandtaxesmag.com, mentalfloss.com, science.howstuffworks.com jumpstartuk.co.uk gizmodo.com